Tynesia Boyea-Robinson operates at the intersection of investing, business, policy, and community-based change. This book is her toolkit to help businesses and organizations across industries work together to create value for all.

—MICHAEL McAFEE
President and CEO, PolicyLink

I met Tynesia as she inaugurated the Washington chapter of Year Up. She was the first person I've ever met who could be both mentor and mentee simultaneously! Her infectious leadership style opened a new chapter in Year Up and infused a spirit of "Good Trouble" in the corporate giving world.

—JOHN KING
Cofounder, Perot Systems Corp

We cannot create an economy that works for all until businesses harness the power of social impact to create a virtuous cycle of investment and equitable growth. *The Social Impact Advantage* has everything you need for your company to contribute to that cycle and reap the benefits.

—DON CHEN
President, Surdna Foundation

Tynesia Boyea-Robinson's new book will give you the tools you need to maximize returns for your company across all dimensions—social, environmental, and financial. Her core insight is that principles of impact investing work best when fully integrated into the way a company's business model is designed and its operations are constructed—becoming "the main course and not just a side dish."

—BRUCE ROSENBLUM
Managing Director, Carlyle

Consumers have made it clear that they want companies to reflect their values, holding businesses to a higher standard that prioritizes both societal and financial outcomes. This book is a roadmap for corporate leaders to be better and do better—strengthening the bottom line along the way.

—DARREN WALKER
President, Ford Foundation

As companies get more involved in the outcomes of their giving and the impact on our world, it's important to understand the shared value of advancing society while enhancing the competitive position of the company. This book gives you the tools and insights you need to operate as a successful business in the 21st century.

—ASHA VARGHESE
President, Caterpillar Foundation

We all crave lives of meaning. We are more engaged professionally when we believe our jobs have purpose. In *The Social Impact Advantage*, the inestimable Ty Boyea-Robinson gives advice to seasoned leaders and up-and-coming professionals alike on how to advocate for and craft this sense of purpose at work.

—JOHN COLEMAN
author of *The HBR Guide to Crafting Your Purpose*

From her experience at NASA, GE, and Year Up, Tynesia Boyea-Robinson shares a formula so simple for how businesses can align their work with impact, it almost seems too good to be true: Innovate, Accelerate, and/or Decelerate. But those are the fundamental options behind all social impact. This book is full of examples and should not be missed!

—CATHY CLARK
Faculty Director of CASE, Duke University

THE
SOCIAL IMPACT
ADVANTAGE

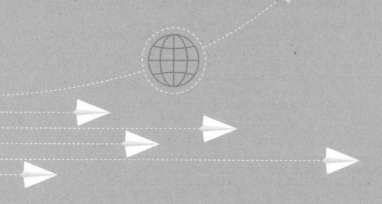

Win Customers and Talent by
Harnessing Your Business for Good

TYNESIA
BOYEA-ROBINSON

Mc
Graw
Hill

New York Chicago San Francisco Athens London Madrid
Mexico City Milan New Delhi Singapore Sydney Toronto

1 2 3 4 5 6 7 8 9   LCR   27 26 25 24 23 22

ISBN   978-1-264-26968-6
MHID   1-264-26968-4

e-ISBN   978-1-264-26969-3
e-MHID   1-264-26969-2

Library of Congress Cataloging-in-Publication Data

Names: Boyea-Robinson, Tynesia, author.
Title: The social impact advantage : win customers and talent by harnessing
   your business for good / Tynesia Boyea-Robinson.
Description: New York, NY : McGraw Hill, [2023] | Includes
   bibliographical references and index.
Identifiers: LCCN 2022028436 (print) | LCCN 2022028437 (ebook) |
   ISBN 9781264269686 (hardback) | ISBN 9781264269693 (ebook)
Subjects: LCSH: Social responsibility of business. | Customer relations. |
   Organizational change.
Classification: LCC HD60 .B69 2023 (print) | LCC HD60 (ebook) |
   DDC 658.4/08—dc23/eng/20220831
LC record available at https://lccn.loc.gov/2022028436
LC ebook record available at https://lccn.loc.gov/2022028437

McGraw Hill books are available at special quantity discounts to use
as premiums and sales promotions or for use in corporate training
programs. To contact a representative, please visit the Contact Us pages
at www.mhprofessional.com.

McGraw Hill is committed to making our products accessible to all
learners. To learn more about the available support and accommodations
we offer, please contact us at accessibility@mheducation.com. We also
participate in the Access Text Network (www.accesstext.org), and
ATN members may submit requests through ATN.

To my Grandma Boyea and to all the other people
who believe a better world is possible.

CONTENTS

FOREWORD

The Future of Business Is Delivering
Value to All Stakeholders

Even before we sold AND 1—the company I co-led with some of my closest friends that grew into a $240 million global basketball apparel, footwear, and entertainment brand—I knew it was time to do something different.

In our decade plus of building a global brand, we learned a lot about how business works. Not just what they teach in MBA classes, but what it actually takes to go from selling T-shirts out of the trunk of a car to competing successfully against Nike and other multibillion dollar businesses with way more resources.

Among other things like smarts, hard work, and luck (and in our case some race, gender, and class advantages I wasn't fully appreciative of at the time), AND 1 was successful because we had a clear purpose that spoke to the hearts of our incredibly talented team. AND 1's mission was to become the number one basketball company in the world. We would accomplish that by being the brand for ballplayers who talked trash and had the game to back it up. People love an underdog, and that was true not only for the 200 people who worked directly for AND 1, but also for our global distributors, suppliers, warehouse and financing partners, retailers, and of course the millions of basketball players who saw themselves (or who they wanted to be on the court) in our brand.

In addition to shared purpose and a great place to work (with a gym, full court hoops, yoga classes, and lots of family-friendly activities), AND 1 shared the upside of building a successful brand with all of our employees through stock options. Following the lead of trailblazers like Patagonia and Ben & Jerry's, AND 1 generated those profits responsibly, primarily by implementing a best-in-class code of conduct for all of our footwear and apparel suppliers, ensuring that the 10,000 young women who worked in our suppliers' factories were paid fairly and treated well in safe and healthy working conditions. AND 1 also donated 5 percent of its net profits, cumulatively more than $2 million, to youth and education programs that benefited our target customers. As a result of this culture and these practices, all of our team members, suppliers, and other partners felt vested in our collective success so they stepped up in various ways to save our company from numerous life-threatening situations.

When we sold AND 1, it didn't take long for the new owner, American Sporting Goods, to gut all of those responsible business practices. ASG turned a stakeholder-driven business into a shareholder-driven business, with only one shareholder. It's not surprising to me that AND 1 as a brand has deteriorated largely into "whatever-happened-to" status, and that AND 1 as a business is no longer a good bet for long-term shareholder value creation because it has been resold at least three or four times, and has likely not produced any meaningful value for the rest of its stakeholders.

My AND 1 experience showed me both the power of delivering value to all your stakeholders and the perils of focusing exclusively on delivering value to shareholders. As I began the mental transition from AND 1, I wanted to find a way to support business leaders and investors seeking to practice this better way of doing business—better for themselves, better for their workers, better for their communities, better for the environment.

Luckily, as with AND 1, I was joined by two of my closest friends—Bart Houlahan, AND 1's president, and Andrew Kassoy, an original AND 1 investor and Wall Street veteran—and together we cofounded the nonprofit B Lab in 2006. B Lab is best known as the certifier of B Corporations, businesses that meet the highest standards of verified social and environmental performance, public transparency, and legal accountability to balance profit and purpose. The "B" stands for the benefit they create for all stakeholders—their customers, workers, suppliers, communities, and the environment. There are now more than 4,600 certified B Corporations across 155 industries and 78 countries, including disruptors who have gone public at billion-dollar valuations like Allbirds and Guild Education, planet- and people-first icons like Patagonia and Ben & Jerry's, and Fortune 500 multinationals like Danone North America and Natura (owner of The Body Shop).

Beyond those businesses who have earned status as certified B Corporations, the innovation that creates legal accountability to balance profit and purpose is now being used by more than 12,000 businesses. This was made possible after B Lab and the community of certified B Corporations helped pass laws in nearly 40 US states, including Delaware, the legal home of the majority of publicly traded companies, and about a half-dozen countries, to create a new corporate structure called a benefit corporation, which upgrades the fiduciary duty of directors to include a requirement to consider the impact of their decisions on all stakeholders, not just shareholders. In one indication of mainstream market acceptance, BlackRock, the world's largest investor with more than $10 trillion in assets under management, recently announced in their 2022 proxy guidance to equity investors that they were generally supportive of management proposals to adopt the benefit corporation's stakeholder governance structure.

I am currently the CEO of Imperative 21, a network of allied organizations, including B Lab, The B Team, CECP

(Chief Executives for Corporate Purpose), Common Future, Conscious Capitalism, the GIIN (Global Impact Investing Network), JUST Capital, and Participant Media, who believe the imperative of the twenty-first century is to transform our economic system so that it can fulfill its higher purpose to create shared well-being on a healthy planet. In short, we work in radical collaboration to shift the narrative about the purpose of business and to accelerate mainstream adoption of stakeholder capitalism as the next normal for business leaders.

This trend toward credible stakeholder capitalism with true accountability for stakeholder performance is accelerating because of rising expectations of customers, workers, and investors. If you want to compete successfully for customers, talent, and capital, you need to do more than talk about purpose, you need to know how to deliver value to all your stakeholders. That's why this new book by Tynesia Boyea-Robinson is so important and useful.

Tynesia Boyea-Robinson (or Ty, as she encourages those who know her to call her) knows what it takes to integrate this stakeholder orientation into day-to-day business decisions about how we as business leaders make money, spend money, and invest in people. Many people talk about stakeholder capitalism, "ESG," "sustainable business," "impact investing," or "social enterprise," but Ty actually knows what's behind this language. As you will read, Ty has collected a career's worth of insights by operating at the intersection of business, government, and nonprofits. She knows what it takes to deliver value to all stakeholders, and this book has everything you need to build a great business by doing the same.

More pointedly, two years into a long overdue racial reckoning, societal expectations to advance racial equity are rising. Through a group I've been involved with since June 2020 called WMRJ (White Men for Racial Justice), I've seen Ty help business leaders learn how to use their positions of power and influence to build businesses and a supportive economic system that work for everyone regardless of where they were born or the color of their skin. With deep insights, contagious passion, and infectious humor, I've seen Ty help business leaders learn how to integrate an equity lens into every business decision, and, importantly, how to respond to understandable concerns that delivering on racial equity will be bad for white people. Ty has helped me and other business leaders see that the opposite is true.

I wish I had had this book 15 years ago when I was starting B Lab, or even better, when I was starting AND 1. I could have avoided many mistakes, and I would have been able to do so much more for my company and our stakeholders so much more quickly.

A stakeholder orientation is better for your business, better for our humanity, and better for society. Proof is everywhere you look: for example, JUST Capital, one of the Imperative 21 network steward organizations, found that public companies who deliver value to all their stakeholders outperformed Russell 1000 Index companies by roughly 30 percent.[1]

As Ty says, your customers—and your current and potential employees—do really want you to be good. You can choose to meet this customer and employee demand and benefit from it, or you can ignore this trend and lose your customers and talent to another business.

I'm glad you are reading this book. Your customers will thank you, your employees will thank you, your investors will thank you, and, most importantly, your children will thank you for showing them what it looks like to live a life with purpose authentically at the center.

JAY COEN GILBERT
entrepreneur and cofounder, AND 1 and B Lab;
CEO, Imperative 21

INTRODUCTION

Harnessing the Power
of the Moonshot Mindset

Not many 16-year-olds get to work at NASA, but there I was: a summer high school intern working at the Kennedy Space Center in Cape Canaveral. I was a part of SHARP (Summer High School Apprenticeship Research Program), working on the International Space Station Alpha (ISSA) initiative, and everywhere I looked were nerds—with pocket protectors, which I didn't even know anyone used. They talked in some kind of unique language, with acronyms for everything, and used words in new ways I didn't understand. It took me several weeks, for example, to realize "payload" was their word for "satellite." The place, as I affectionately refer to it now, was a total nerd oasis. And I loved it!

My first day there, they gave me a thick folder containing packets and booklets with the straightforward name of "Information Kit." It contained massive amounts of paper—yes, it was so long ago it was printed on paper—and contained things like the Kennedy Space Center strategic plan, a map of the series of buildings I had to navigate, a SHARP student handbook, and other documents that would help me understand what my job was and how I should do it. I lugged this "kit" around with me every day that summer.

I spent my first days looking through this information to learn as fast as I could what was happening around me. One particularly helpful item was a thick little book that contained all those acronyms—things like VAB, or the "vehicle assembly building," which was the building where they put the space shuttle together. (Well, the book wasn't that little, but it fit in my purse.) Whenever anyone used an acronym, I rushed to find out what it meant before someone used another. Part of my job was to take notes and measurements as my team worked to open a new building to support the construction of the space station. The project was massive—we were literally working to put someone into space. Hard to believe that was me working at the place that put a man on the moon. It was at the same time humbling and inspiring.

TWO ESSENTIALS FOR ACHIEVING YOUR GOALS: AMBITION AND PROCESS

I learned two important lessons working with nerds. First, I was a nerd too. I had always been nerd-curious, focused on my studies and gravitating toward the sciences. But, as a young Black woman, I wasn't able to identify with nerd culture. A nerd was a skinny white man, not a short Black girl. After working at NASA, I knew there was a place for me among the nerds. This insight helped me take every other step in my life—from studying engineering and computer science in college to working in e-commerce at GE, and even running a technology-focused nonprofit a decade later.

The second lesson I learned was related to that nondescript Information Kit: everything was so complex, but that didn't mean everything had to be overwhelming. To my teenage mind lugging that kit around with me each day seemed burdensome, but it actually represented a distillation of the massive amount of logistical information and processes that went into building

FIGURE I.1 The author at NASA

the space station. That manual walked me through all the possible complexities, from what certain acronyms meant to a process that would lead to discoveries, like how to assemble pieces in a way that would eventually create a machine that could sustain human life in space. While our goal was a literal moonshot, we had step-by-step plans that helped us build our shared vision. From the lowliest intern (me) to the most senior leader, we were undeterred by aiming for what had never been done and motivated by what we could create together.

There were thousands of people working to launch International Space Station Alpha into space, all with various tasks and responsibilities. And each task, every step, was coordinated and integrated—even something as small as my measurement tasks—to achieve a broader, bold goal. Though my Information Kit may have seemed a burden at the time, I know now it was just as critical to the overall success of the shuttle launch as the external tank and boosters that propelled the

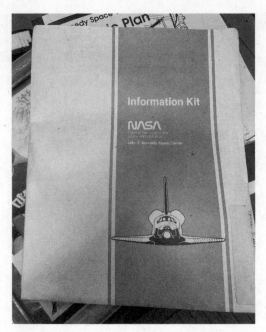

FIGURE I.2 The author's NASA Information Kit

astronauts into space, or the oxygen that kept them alive. It was a part of a broader system of checklists and meeting structures and procedures that together led to the bold action of sending a person into space. Achieving bold results requires a moon-shot mindset, but also an information kit (or two or three). We tend to forget this when we are building businesses or trying to change society. When people achieve big things, they are called "visionaries" because of their big ideas. Steve Jobs brought us the personal computer through his genius. Albert Einstein brought us a whole new way to think about the universe. Martin Luther King Jr. inspired a nation to change. But while those men were visionaries, they also had hundreds and sometimes thousands of people working with them to achieve their big, bold goal.

This dual appreciation of both the mindset and what it takes to achieve that mindset is missing from much of our work in business and society. We may focus too much on the end goal and not enough on setting the right targets to help us get there. We may have big ideas but be unable to execute on them (or undervalue the work that it takes to achieve them) because we lack the information kit that will lead the way to getting there.

If we can recognize and harness the power of both the moonshot mindset and the information kits it takes, we can build anything. We can change how we do business. We can change the world.

FROM NASA TO GE: MOONSHOT MINDSET AT WORK IN A BLUE-CHIP CORPORATION

My first job out of school was as an analyst at GE. GE was rapidly expanding then, acquiring companies left and right they felt would be a good fit for the company. Some of the aspects of the business seemed ludicrous. During my time there, I analyzed credit card services, mortgage banking, and the manufacture of locomotive engine parts. Looking back, the expansive and seemingly ridiculous portfolio of the fictional GE's vice president of East Coast Television, Jack Donaghy, from the TV show *30 Rock,* was not very different from how the company operated.

But as a young analyst at GE, I soon learned that while the products and services of GE's different business units might seem incongruous, there was always a common thread that tied everything together: process and culture. Their information kits were essentially the same, regardless of what you were working on. We received endless PowerPoint slides that walked us through any process—from acquiring a $2 million business to managing a team—supplemented with support from senior leaders and relentless training to build GE's version of "moonshot mindset" culture, which at the time translated to "be the best or leave." This symbiosis of process and culture led to a high-performing workforce that didn't shy away from thinking big, or doing what it took to execute on those big, bold plans.

I was successful at GE. I became a Six Sigma Black Belt, learning the famed process improvement tools and techniques to help our business units grow and succeed at whatever we tried to do, whether it was an acquisition of a mortgage bank in Mexico or the rollout of new engine products for a high-speed train. I learned a lot in college, but at GE I was able to apply what I learned and see what I could achieve. I was making more money than my parents did, and I was on a trajectory to lead a business division in a short amount of time. So I did what most people in my position would have done: I went to business school to try to get to that next level.

It's here where normally you would read about how there was one moment where I stopped and looked around at my life and realized that I wasn't fulfilled in my corporate job. That I needed to give back and help others more than I was doing in a big, faceless multinational company. I will admit, as a Black woman and the first in my immediate family to go to college, there were moments where I asked myself, "Whom did I leave behind to be successful? Whom did I betray or abandon?" I was mindful of the platform I had as one of the few Black women in GE, and I held some responsibility to do more because of that.

But, when I went off to graduate school, I fully expected to return to GE and run an international business unit, continuing on my path. I was happy where I was, and I knew that I was achieving big, bold things. But after a unique opportunity at business school, I realized that by using the tools and techniques I had learned at NASA and GE, I could aim for an even bigger moonshot.

SHIFTING GEARS: MOONSHOT MINDSET AT WORK IN A NATIONAL NONPROFIT

My summer internship at business school was to support a growing national nonprofit, Year Up, as they developed a business and expansion plan. Year Up worked with young people who had graduated from high school but did not have many opportunities after that. They put them through training to receive college credits and set them up with apprenticeships in technology companies to help with project management, IT, and other tasks. I knew I could be of help because these kids were essentially preparing for my first job at GE.

I must admit, I fell in love with Year Up. I saw myself and my family in every young person who walked through the doors. My summer project was to provide data on which regions of the country would be best targeted for expansion out of the Boston area, and the board was deciding between the DC area and New York City. After I delivered my analysis to the board at Year Up, I thought I was done with the organization and it was back to GE for me. In the end, I am grateful that the founder, Gerald Chertavian—a successful tech entrepreneur and Wall Street banker—had other ideas.

The board ended up deciding on DC over New York City. With this decision made, Gerald called me into his office one day with a proposition: once I graduated from business school, he asked me to come work with him as the founding executive director of the first national expansion into the DC area.

I thought about it and realized I couldn't pass it up. These young adults were dealing with some of the hardest challenges a person could face in life—many of them were working to provide for their families while trying to educate themselves and get a better job. Some had unstable housing situations and traveled hours by public transit just to get to work. They were not seen as the "typical" corporate employee, but Gerald and his team were working to change that.

Creating the environment where talented and often overlooked youth could amass the experiences they needed to succeed seemed, to some, too daunting and impossible to achieve. But, because of what I had learned at GE and what I had seen at NASA, I knew that it wasn't. The process was complicated, but it was doable. It just required the right information kits.

Yet setting up and establishing these processes and procedures was harder than what I had experienced at GE or even NASA. We were tackling problems that wouldn't be fixed by reinforcing structures with different types of metal, or through different lines of code. We were working to support youth who faced barriers to success that were deeply ingrained in the structure of our society. It required working with people to change their perceptions of who these young people were and to give them a chance they wouldn't have otherwise.

Despite these challenges, I raised over $20 million and we grew from placing 22 students in internships at 8 companies to placing over 1,000 students at over 40 internship partners, including the White House. I was one proud momma. Who wouldn't be? But one morning, after seven years, I pulled up outside of our nondescript offices on Wilson Boulevard in Northern Virginia. I looked up at the windows to the second floor of the office building where our staff was already working away. We had new hills to climb, more young people to serve, and more important work to do. And then I was hit by an unshakeable feeling: I was not the one to take us there.

THE NEXT MOONSHOT: HARNESSING THE POWER OF SOCIAL IMPACT

Where did this feeling come from? I wanted to do the work at Year Up, because, in part, I knew that the young adults we were helping were like me and my family. I came from a jumbled background of opportunity and disadvantage. On my dad's side, my grandparents were from Guyana and Japan; my mom's family was Black from Long Beach, California. My father was the youngest of five children and his brothers and sisters are traditionally successful—teacher, banker, marketing executive, engineer. As a teenage father, instead of going to college, my dad joined the military in order to support his young family. Meanwhile, my mom (and later my stepmom as well) came from families where no one had ever gone to college, women often had babies young, and everyone pitched in to raise the children.

All of these factors shaped who I am today. My aunts and uncles and my paternal grandmother provided a lot of my initial upbringing. They took me to libraries and museums, where I discovered that the world was full of potential and possibility; they instilled in me the importance of education that would stay with me for the rest of my life. My dad's family showed me that there's a big world out there, and I was always looking for new opportunities to learn and grow. In contrast, my mother taught me to find joy and laughter in the midst of sadness and to trust and believe in the good in the world even when you have been hurt by those closest to you. My father and stepmom taught me discipline and responsibility. Under their roof, I learned to work hard, admit my mistakes, and channel my gifts toward something bigger than myself. As the firstborn child, niece, and granddaughter, I was given my first and best opportunity—the commitment, support, and love of a diverse family structure.

What ran consistently through all of my diverse familial upbringing was a headstrong notion that things can change if you push hard enough. My parents and their families were always pushing to secure a better life for me and my siblings, and they never accepted the idea that how life was is what it had to be. This belief laid the foundation for what would become my moonshot mindset and set me on the path to my career. It pushed me to learn as much as I could and try as hard as I could.

If my professional experiences gave me the information kits I needed to get things done, it was my family that first instilled within me the moonshot mindset that helped me set my sights on what I wanted to achieve and to always go big.

So, when I sat in my car in front of the Year Up offices on Wilson Boulevard, it was this belief in change and my ability to do more that pushed me to move on. Year Up was well on its way to achieving its moonshot, but I knew that there was something else I needed to work on—my own moonshot.

What I had seen at NASA, GE, and Year Up was that the fundamental process for change was the same, no matter if that was a big change or something smaller. The work of assembling an engine for a train has the same fundamental components as trying to put someone into space, it just requires a different set of resources and scope of work.

So I asked myself, while sitting in my car in front of the Year Up office, if I knew how to achieve big things, why shouldn't I set my sights higher? Why not try to hit a bigger moon, higher in the sky?

CHANGING HOW THE WORLD DOES BUSINESS

During my time at Year Up, I saw what it took to achieve substantive, positive changes in the lives of people who needed them. At GE, I had seen what a company could do with the right processes and ambition to create a hugely successful business. I knew that the process behind both of those things was essentially the same.

Yet I also saw that there was a "siloed" nature between the world of business and work that had social impact. Part of the reason I was so successful and raised so much money at Year Up was because I was able to seamlessly move between the business world and the scrappy, out-in-the-streets nonprofit world. And while I was leading Year Up-National Capital Region, I was out in the streets talking to anyone who would listen.

There wasn't a corporate boardroom or wine-and-cheese gala I hadn't attended. I connected with the corporate leaders in DC, many of whom were the people behind the first dot-com boom, because I could speak their language and translate what we were trying to do through Year Up and why they should support it. But oftentimes, after I left those large houses in the Virginia suburbs and took off my high heels for the drive home, it astounded me that I needed a translator. Year Up's work was about creating opportunity for young people and breaking down the barriers that society has set up for them. These geniuses of the internet were also breaking down barriers and creating opportunities; the difference was that they did it with technology. We were talking about the same things, so why didn't we all speak the same language?

The reason for this divide between business outcomes and social outcomes is longstanding and deep-seated in our Western capitalist society. We have been living in an era defined by the Milton Friedman's maxim "the business of business is business." Business leaders see their role as maximizing profit and creating the most value for their customers, employees, and shareholders. Why should they be concerned with anything else? With these profits, the corporate leaders who maximize profits can then choose to give their funds away to help improve society.

This division of labor among the sectors has been essentially unchanged since the first major era of philanthropy began with people like J.D. Rockefeller and Andrew Carnegie. But we are beginning to see those walls come down. Consumers are looking more and more toward businesses to be social and political leaders,[2] and companies are facing increased pressure from boycotts and digital organizing to make statements in support of or against social causes.[3] The millennial generation, in particular, is more interested in civic engagement and giving back and is making consumption decisions based on those values.[4]

Yet businesses continue to treat social impact as a "side dish" rather than the main course of their operations. I saw this working with companies through Year Up. Some saw our work with them as a charitable act—something they were doing *to* our students to help out "disadvantaged youth." Few saw it for what it really was, or could be—a talent recruitment tool to gain highly qualified staff with a high probability for long-term retention.

Year Up was offering something that broke down the silo between business and nonprofits. It gave companies a chance to improve their bottom line while also improving society. Time and time again I saw this offer accepted, but without companies understanding what it really meant for them. I knew that until the business community saw things like Year Up for what they really were—a true win-win—we would not only fail to solve society's biggest challenges, but also fail to unleash the true power of business and the capitalist engine that drives it.

As I sat that day in front of the Year Up offices on Wilson Boulevard, I knew that I had a new challenge to tackle. I began to formulate a new moonshot in my mind: to change how the world does business.

WHAT YOU'LL GAIN FROM
THE SOCIAL IMPACT ADVANTAGE

As you explore the book, it's important to keep in mind that:

- Achieving big things requires two components: an ambitious mindset and processes to achieve your goals.
- Businesses do not meet their full potential because they are unable to recognize social issues as an opportunity to grow and expand.
- Businesses can unlock their full potential by responding to increasing pressure from consumers and employees to respond to social trends.

I certainly have not yet achieved my bold moonshot, but I now see changing how the world does business as my life's work. I and those who have joined with me in this goal have made strong moves, and I am hopeful that we can continue to unlock the true potential of business to both solve problems and generate profit.

Over the years, through my impact investment and advisory firm, CapEQ, I have helped dozens of companies change their practices to improve their bottom line while also improving society. I've worked with major industry players like Walmart, the Carlyle Group, Athleta, and others to help them leverage the power of social impact—or what I'll define in the next chapter more specifically as "equitable impact"—and engage with their customers. I have seen what businesses can do when you no longer think of impact as a side dish, but the main course.

Year Up is an excellent example of this. In the past decade, Year Up has expanded to over 250 companies, including over 40 of the Fortune 100.[5] They have an 85 percent retention rate, and their graduates have achieved an over 50 percent wage gain six to nine months after graduation.[6]

There are more ways businesses can leverage opportunities like Year Up to unlock their full potential while also responding to increasing pressure from consumers and employees to respond to social trends. In this book I provide the lessons I've distilled from more than a decade working with Fortune 500 clients, government agencies, philanthropies, and others to help change the way the world does business. Like the International Space Station, doing this may seem daunting, but following this simple process can get you on your way.

This book provides the lessons distilled from more than a decade of work with Fortune 500 clients, government agencies, philanthropies, and others to help change the way the world does business. To change how you do business and unlock your business's full potential, consider changes in these three areas:

1. How you make money
2. How you spend money
3. How you invest in your people

Chapter by chapter, you will not only discover why these three changes are vital to unlocking the potential in your company, but also how to implement these changes to create your own information kit and foster a moonshot mindset. Here's what you'll find:

- **Chapter 1:** Why Your Customers Want You to Be Good, and What You Can Do About It. This chapter is an overview of why customers want you to be good, and the three areas businesses can consider to respond to modern social and environmental challenges. It will also provide context for why these shifts are needed today as the business climate continues to shift based on consumer and employee preferences.
- **Chapter 2:** Achieving Equitable Impact Through Your Business Model. Businesses are increasingly being held to certain social standards and values by consumers. By shifting consumer-facing activities to align with these values, your business can increase consumer acquisition and revenue.
- **Chapter 3:** Achieving Equitable Impact Through Your Spending. Most companies do not consider their spending as an opportunity for strengthening their bottom line or creating impact. Yet working and partnering with under-resourced and underfunded companies, such as Black-owned businesses, can provide untapped value.
- **Chapter 4:** Achieving Equitable Impact by Investing in Your People. Staffing and talent acquisition are some of the largest ongoing challenges for businesses. Investing in your employees and finding new talent pools to tap into can increase employee retention and productivity. Offering unique benefits can also reduce turnover.
- **Chapter 5:** Build Your CapEQ™ to Make an Equitable Impact. This chapter offers an overview of the CapEQ™ continuum, which provides a granular assessment of how

well companies are equipped to implement the ideas in the book. It will also give specific examples of companies along the continuum.

- **Conclusion:** Changing How YOU Do Business. Here, I summarize the other chapters and conclude by calling on you to implement the recommendations provided in the book and to join a community of practitioners online.

Throughout these chapters, you will find case studies and resources to help you and your team apply the lessons to your business. There is also data and trend analysis to help you make the case to yourself, your boss, or your team for why to remain competitive equitable impact should be the "main course" of your operations. Grounding all of these chapters is what I call the "Good Business Worksheet," which will help you apply what you have learned directly to your company. You can complete this worksheet by yourself, but I recommend you do it with your team to help you get agreement as to the best ways to harness the full potential of your business through equitable impact. If you do the worksheet as a team, I've included some sample agendas to help you facilitate a conversation.

Although the primary audience for this book is those working at for-profit companies, there is advice for anyone looking to change organizational practices and improve society, with particular relevance for investors (individual, philanthropic, or institutional) as well as government officials looking to engage differently with companies. If you want to skip around, I recommend investors start with Chapter 3 and those who work at a government agency or nonprofit start with Chapter 4.

If you are an entrepreneur looking to start a business— welcome! I'm so glad you are using this book so early in the life of your business. Using these tools from the beginning can help you instill the practice of creating equitable impact throughout all aspects of your company. You'll want to start with Chapter 2 to ground your business model in these concepts.

Chapter 3 will be relevant as you ramp up your supply chain, and Chapter 4 will become important as you start to hire your first employees.

Let's get started!

Why Your Customers Want You to Be Good, and What You Can Do About It

The last week of May into the first week of June 2020, similar images kept popping up in my social media feed. Major companies were tweeting out images of white text on all-black backgrounds. As I kept scrolling, more kept popping up: Amazon, Disney, TikTok, the NFL, Marvel. Even video game companies like EA Sports and PlayStation had their own versions.

These white text/black background images were, of course, responses to the murder of George Floyd and in support of racial justice. The collective despair and anguish that we all felt while watching the 8-minute, 46-second video of Floyd's death shocked this country into an uprising not seen in a generation. People place a lot of trust in companies, and, as a result, expect more from them. They want the companies and brands they support to authentically engage with social causes and create equitable impact. Companies could not choose to be silent on this issue as millions of people (and potential customers) took to the streets protesting the systemic racism Black people and people of color face each day. In the social media age, companies large and small quickly shared their thoughts and responses, with many also pledging dollars to racial justice charities.

But while social media allowed companies to connect quickly with people during this emotionally charged time, the digital nature of the communication allowed consumers to connect right back with them. Many people saw these statements as hollow and nothing more than a PR opportunity with a little money thrown in for good measure.[1] The statements became so ubiquitous and mocked that one Twitter user created a standard [Brand] response template (see Figure 1.1).

FIGURE 1.1 A standard [brand] response

Like many things on social media the outcry in response to these statements quickly ebbed. But some of these statements of support were met with more than an eye roll and snark. There were real consequences, with some companies' statements being called out as hypocritical in light of past decisions that were seen as racist.

When the beauty company L'Oréal released a statement in support of the Black community and encouraged their customers to speak out against racism, the model Munroe Bergdorf shared that when working on a L'Oréal campaign in 2017 she was fired because she spoke out about white privilege after the white supremacist rally in Charlottesville that left a counter-protestor dead. In her response to L'Oréal's statement in solidarity with the racial justice protests in 2020, she said:

> I had to fend for myself being torn apart by the world's press because YOU didn't want to talk about racism. You do NOT get to do this. This is NOT okay, not even in the slightest. . . . Where was my support when I spoke out?

A company's reputation and brand value were not the only things that suffered in the backlash to some of their statements. The most notable example occurred at the food magazine *Bon Appétit*, whose editor-in-chief resigned in June 2020 when current and former employees raised allegations of racial discrimination and a toxic work environment. Several other senior-level departures followed, and the magazine had to pause and rebuild one of their most popular revenue streams, their YouTube channel, which had over six million followers and was one of the largest video outlets for parent company Condé Nast. Many of their biggest stars refused to continue to work with *Bon Appétit* because of its unfair treatment of people of color.[2]

Nevertheless, the deluge of corporate statements in response to the death of George Floyd were an encouraging step forward and represented a shift in our culture. The NFL went from banning players for kneeling during the national anthem to protest police brutality[3] to releasing a statement that included the words "black lives matter." But, the callouts and accusations of inauthenticity also showed that companies needed not only to think more about and be better at navigating the current social landscape, but to do more not just when something happened that caused a public outcry.

Many companies did, though, "walk the walk" and followed through on the commitments they made in the summer of 2020. Citibank, for example, made a $1 billion commitment toward closing the gap in wealth between Black people and white people—which by some measures is a 10 times difference on average between the races[4]—and committed to deploying these funds to increase homeownership rates, support Black businesses, and partner with nonprofits working on racial equity. As of the fall of 2021, Citi was meeting or exceeding their goals,[5] leveraging some of the strategies outlined in this book, such as using procurement dollars to support Black-owned business suppliers.

Citibank and the other examples I'll share show that engaging with social causes can no longer end with a company sending out a statement and donating some money. Customers expect that what you say is consistent with what you do and who you are as a company. That means it'll take a lot more work to meet the needs of those customers than simply putting some words on a black background every time something major happens around the world.

WHY YOUR COMPANY SHOULD CARE (OR THE BUSINESS OF BUSINESS IS NOT JUST BUSINESS)

At this point, you are probably saying to yourself—OK lady, I hear you, but didn't these same companies post record profits in 2020?[6] Seems like they are doing something right.

And you would be correct. Many of these companies did exceedingly well during the aftermath of George Floyd's death (and the height of the pandemic), and continue to do well. PR fiascos come and go, and companies putting their feet in their mouths isn't anything new to this century.

But dismissing the challenges companies had navigating the events of the summer of 2020 ignores a broader trend in customer behavior that companies cannot afford to dismiss. People place a lot of trust in companies, and expect more because of it. The Edelman Trust Barometer, an annual survey of trust and credibility, shows that despite the economic turmoil of the past few decades, trust in business has only continued to rise, and now businesses are more trusted than both government and nonprofits (referred to as NGOs or "nongovernmental organizations"). Trust in businesses has grown in the age 35–64 demographic by 17 percentage points since 2007, and in 2018, for the first time, businesses were more trusted than NGOs.[7]

But this trust also comes with expectations from customers. Almost 90 percent of Edelman survey respondents said that all stakeholders—customers, employees, *and* communities—are most important to a company's long-term success. Only a little more than 10 percent say that shareholders are the most important thing. Over 70 percent agree that "a company can take specific actions that both increase profits and improve the economic and social conditions in which it operates."[8]

These trends are even more apparent in the growing-in-influence millennial population. Millennials were 1.5 times more likely to purchase a product from a "sustainable" brand, and twice as likely to look for a job at a sustainably minded company.[9] Over 70 percent of millennials say that giving back and being civically engaged are their highest priorities.[10]

Women, too, tend to be more focused on companies who are doing well BY doing good. Research on sustainable investing conducted by Morgan Stanley found that around 80 percent of women say they are interested in socially responsible investing, and 56 percent were interested in their investments having a positive impact, compared to 45 percent of men.[11]

And these consumers can smell BS too. Anything hypocritical will be called out. Authenticity is more important than anything else. Consumer research has shown that up to 90 percent of consumers say that authenticity is an important factor in determining which brands they like and support,[12] and companies that improve their reputations can increase their sales by up to three times.[13]

A focus on social causes and social impact adds up to an increased customer base and additional profits: Research from Neilsen found that two-thirds of consumers say they prefer to buy from companies that create social impact, and nearly half say they are willing to pay more to do so.[14]

Despite some of the corporate missteps in the wake of George Floyd's murder—and the backlash that came from both the political left and the right—consumers have actually doubled-down on their expectations for companies since 2020. In their 2021 survey, Edelman found that businesses have much more to gain than lose by taking a stand on racial injustice. Over 80 percent of consumers say a company would gain or earn their trust by doing so, a four-percentage-point increase from 2020. In 2021, there was a 20 percent increase in the number of people who said they would start or stop using a brand based on a company's response to the racial justice protests. These increases were most pronounced among younger consumers.[15]

Given all this, and with all due respect to Milton Friedman, it is clear that the business of business is not just business. A focus only on profit maximization is not what your customers want, and continuing that shareholder-driven approach is costing you customers and revenue.

Convincing Your Boss

If you're in charge—either of a team or of a company—
implementing the recommendations I describe in this book
will be easier than if you need buy-in from your manager to
integrate equitable impact as a core part of the business.
Often younger or mid-career professionals are the ones
pushing to take on more social impact initiatives, and it's
the (older) senior leadership that needs to be convinced.

I'm often asked the best way to convince someone in a
leadership position the value of doing well BY doing good.
This is a hard question to answer—so much depends on
the person and what motivates him or her. Of course, the
easiest way to sell them on these recommendations is to
give them the book! But, if for some reason they don't want
to read my book (gasp!), the data outlined below can be a
strong part of any pitch you may be making to your boss,
or your boss's boss.

In my experience, the most compelling attention
grabbers are:

- Two-thirds of consumers say they prefer to buy from
  companies that create social impact.

- Nearly half say they are willing to pay more to do so.

- Ninety percent say that all stakeholders—customers,
  employees, and communities—are most important to a
  company's long-term success.[16]

If you find yourself in an elevator with your CEO, use
this data as a part of your 30-second pitch.

CAPITALISM'S "HOLY TRINITY": CREATING EQUITABLE IMPACT

Our country was founded on the belief that "all men are created equal." Yet, not every American was included. Not even every American man was included. What ultimately was most dangerous about the dichotomy between the ideals of our country's founding—as understood then—and the reality of the laws the founders put in place—as they were applied over time—is that it led to a belief in a fair system where everyone had the ability to win. This belief held despite not everyone being able to participate in, much less compete in, what became our American capitalist system. And with each generation, Americans of means pass on a belief to their children that they are winning because they earned it, because they worked hard, because they fought the good fight. What they do not acknowledge is that generation after generation they have had a head start through unfair accumulation of wealth that assures them victory.

It is easy to think rigging the fight was only a problem in the early days of American capitalism. But that's not so. Coupled with continued racist policies, the capitalist system has been rigged against working people and especially people of color since the country began up to and including now. The most egregious failure of American capitalism was slavery, which many of the country's founders believed was not only an economic necessity, but righteous. Others accepted this view without question. Its legacy is felt today. Enslaved Americans did not have the freedom to benefit from the goods they produced nor the resulting profit—up to $59 trillion by some estimates.[17] Even after slavery was abolished, the country moved on to Jim Crow, then redlining, and on to the GI Bill and the Social Security Act, which also deliberately excluded people of color. More recently, the Federal Highway Act and Urban Renewal calculatedly destroyed Black communities, and predatory loans and mortgages were explicitly targeted at Black and brown people.

From day one, American capitalism violated the very tenets of freedom and opportunity espoused by the system. And the results show: according to Opportunity Insights, a nonpartisan, not-for-profit organization based at Harvard University, if you are born in the United States, your zip code is a greater predictor of your success than your substance, particularly if you are a person of color.[18]

But despite these failings, capitalism as an economic system is not inherently good or evil. It is just a tool for organizing a society and culture. What is more important than the tool is the people and how and why they wielded that tool. Historically, despite our country's ideals, the underlying belief of those in power in human inferiority has undermined the system and justified unfair practices.

It doesn't have to continue that way. The promise of our country and the freedom that we espouse has consistently attracted dreamers, problem solvers, hard workers, and all manner of geniuses from across the globe. Our ideals have inspired people from all backgrounds to bring their talents to our shores and often transform our country and the world for the better.

American companies represent 80 percent[19] of the world's top companies as defined by market capitalization. In addition, over half of the Fortune top 25 best global companies to work for are headquartered in the United States.[20] And perhaps, unsurprisingly, several companies appear on both lists. Most people tout market capitalization as the ultimate indicator of economic health, but the most recent financial downturns show that profit at the expense of people and the planet have longstanding negative externalities which are now amplified due to our global interconnectedness—such as financial products leading to market instability or a disregard of the social costs of carbon dioxide production leading to increased pollution. However, the fact that so many US companies are considered great places to work is an indicator that these organizations have the raw material in place to aspire to the next level of shared prosperity.

Central to this shared prosperity is an investment in our common infrastructure, both physical and social. Many people hear "American capitalism" and think "make as much money as you can no matter the cost," but that idea is relatively recent. Immediately after World War II, companies were more likely to invest in infrastructure, talent, education, and other resources that all communities and businesses benefited from—there was little difference between prosperity of a business and the communities it worked in. According to professors Jan Rivken and Michael Porter, as globalization trends separated a business's location from its workforce, a disconnect between business and communities developed and led to divestment in collective resources.[21]

We now see that investments in physical and social capital are not "nice-to-have" measures; instead, many are the very factors that drive economic resilience. Although there is more work to be done to address the oftentimes crumbling infrastructure in the United States (both human and physical), American capitalism has a longstanding culture of looking to stabilize environments to create the enabling conditions required to facilitate resilient commerce.

Despite the many challenges to our economic approach, American capitalism works well for those for whom it works. So the question is: How do we both harness the strength of our current approach and acknowledge historical and existing inequity to help businesses access their full potential and help strengthen our American capitalist system? How do we help businesses create what I call "equitable impact"?

We have to get back to that pre–World War II approach to capitalism with what I call the "holy trinity of capitalism." This trinity is comprised of (1) a business owner, who creates something of value, (2) a customer, who pays for that value, and (3) businesses, that hire employees to produce that value in exchange for a livable wage and a quality standard of living. That holy trinity has been disrupted over the years, as people focused more on profit maximization, cutting costs by reducing wages and benefits paid to employees, and cutting the quality of the products and services delivered to the customer. The result: cheaper goods of lower quality and full-time employees who must rely on government assistance to make ends meet.

To restore the holy trinity of capitalism, we have to get back to the true meaning of "value." Often the theoretical idea of "value" in business is shorthanded as "profit." This makes sense in some ways, if someone is willing to pay you more for a product or service than what you put into it assumes you have added value to whatever you are selling. Sometimes, it is that simple. But on a broader, economic scale, equating profit with value is deeply flawed. At the beginning of the chapter, I discussed corporations whose stock prices rose during the pandemic, increasing profits for their shareholders. It would be hard to argue that the overall value added to the country by these companies was equivalent to the increase in their stock prices during a time of great suffering and pain.

My friend and colleague Jay Coen Gilbert has focused his post–AND 1 career on this idea of redefining what corporate value creation should be (see his Foreword for more detail). Rather than focusing on short-term profit for shareholders, we have to think about total value-add for all *stakeholders*—from the quality of life of workers to the health of customers and the well-being of the people living in our neighborhoods and communities. Some of this value creation is measurable—such as the health of people in a community, or the ability of employees to afford rent and groceries—but some of it is intangible; for example, whether or not a company is being a good partner in creating a better life for everyone it touches. Jay believes, as do I, that this stakeholder-not-shareholder perspective on business is actually aligned with the core fundamentals of our democratic capitalist system.

Larry Fink, the CEO of the massive investment management company BlackRock, also agrees. In his 2022 annual letter to all CEOs of companies in which BlackRock invests, he said:

> Stakeholder capitalism is not about politics. It is not a social or ideological agenda. It is not "woke." *It is capitalism*, driven by mutually beneficial relationships between you and the employees, customers, suppliers, and communities your company relies on to *prosper*. This is the power of capitalism.[22]

Instead of focusing on profit and shareholders, we must consider all stakeholders and the value transfer that happens at all levels of a company's behavior, not just at the point of sale between customer and business. This broader consideration of how a business is creating value will expand your priorities as a business owner or employee, and help ground your work in that holy trinity of what capitalism should be—creating impact that benefits all stakeholders in an equitable way. It will create a virtuous cycle of value-add activities that will help your employees and contractors have a quality standard of living and your customers have an enjoyable experience—while maximizing your profits. Leveraging capitalism in this way can create equitable impact that benefits all; in fact, it is so essential to how I do business that I named my company after it: CapEQ, a mash-up of capitalism and equitable impact.

So, maybe our good friend Milton Friedman wasn't wrong, just a little off: the business of business IS business, we just need to rethink how we do business and what we can achieve with the tools of capitalism. We need to refocus on true value-generation and increasing overall well-being instead of profit maximization, and not get distracted by the "winner take all" mentality we have now. Achieving the true potential for your business, and all businesses, requires us to shift our mindset to think about profit and value in this way.

FINDING AUTHENTICITY WITH THE EQUITABLE IMPACT VENN DIAGRAM

Easier said than done, right? Taking these steps is hard work, but necessary. With this changing sociopolitical environment, businesses ignore engaging in social causes at their peril. Sooner or later, they will be pulled into some social discourse, either by their consumers or their employees. The past few years—with our increasingly fraught political environment around racial justice, climate change, voting rights, and other activist causes—show that companies need to be prepared.

We know that inauthentic, performative, one-time statements aren't enough. This work needs to be embedded across a company, encompassing all stakeholders, including the broader community. These changes need to be long-term and sustained.

For example, the Dove "Campaign for Real Beauty" turned traditional beauty advertising on its head to highlight "real" women and their bodies rather than photoshopped models representing unrealistic standards of beauty. The campaign began in 2004 and has been massively successful (I am sure you have seen some of the ads), helping to shift industry standards, elevate different types of beauty, and increase engagement with customers in an authentic way. The Campaign for Real Beauty was one of the first ad campaigns that benefited from social media and the desire of people to share the content themselves because it aligned with their identity and values.[23]

Nevertheless, this campaign and the broader body positive movement has received some sustained criticism. Namely, as the writer Amanda Mull laid out, it shames women for feeling bad about beauty standards that companies like Dove and others behind those ads helped create without the companies acknowledging their own part in creating those unreasonable expectations and the pain that goes along with them.[24] On the other hand, it also shows the potential for what a business can achieve when it thinks differently and works to integrate social causes across its operations.

Contrariwise, what does this look like when the commitment is performative and not sustained? Well, you may remember some big news out of the Business Roundtable a few years ago. The Roundtable, an association for the executives of some of the country's biggest companies, released a statement in 2019 with over 150 cosigners that "redefined the purpose of the corporation to promote an 'economy that serves all Americans,'" and said "we share a fundamental commitment to all of our stakeholders," not just shareholders.[25]

Well OK then! Problem solved, right? Not so fast. When put to the test, many of these companies went back on their commitments and suffered as a result. As research from Wharton Professor Tyler Wry found, when the COVID-19 pandemic hit, the stakeholder pledge signers gave 20 percent more of their profits to shareholders as compared to companies who did not sign the pledge.[26] This led them to be "almost 20 percent more prone to announce layoffs or furloughs. Signers were less likely to donate to relief efforts, less likely to offer customer discounts, and less likely to shift production to pandemic-related goods."[27]

We can't know for sure why these companies did not follow through on their pledge, but, in an interview with *The Atlantic* writer Jerry Useem, Professor Wry suggested that it may have a fundamentally psychological reason: "If people are allowed to make a token gesture of moral behavior—or simply imagine they've done *something* good—they then feel freer to do something morally dubious, because they've reassured themselves that they're on the side of the angels."[28]

This book is designed to help you avoid this type of behavior. It is easy to make a quick promise and put out a statement, but it's harder to stay committed and follow through. It requires taking a hard look at your practices and considering your business practices differently. If you can't do that and be committed to the equitable impact you want to create, you will be seen as inauthentic and won't be able to engage with your customers in the way they want you to. Your "authenticity" has to be real, not performative. In many cases, achieving this authentic, long-term engagement means overhauling certain practices or developing a new operating philosophy.

Defining the authentic, unique equitable impact your company can create is both very simple and incredibly complex. You find it at the intersection of three elements:

1. Your organizational passion and values
2. The root cause of the issue you are trying to solve
3. The assets you can bring to the issue

These are the components of the Equitable Impact Venn Diagram I use to help clients find their sweet spot for equitable impact (see Figure 1.2).

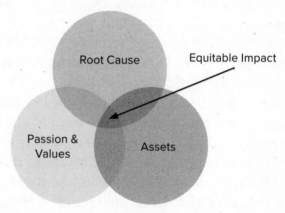

FIGURE 1.2 The Equitable Impact Venn Diagram

Looking at this Venn diagram, you probably could come up with an off-the-cuff statement about each of the elements and the equitable impact you could create. Your root cause issue might be a lack of good jobs in a community; your passion and values might be creating a welcoming and inclusive workplace; and your assets might be a franchise business model that creates entry-level job openings. Your equitable impact would be something around investing in the communities in which your business operates.

But the process for creating and defining what this equitable impact actually looks like is where things get complex. You can very quickly feel as if you need to do everything! Your business touches so many aspects of society, it's hard not to get overwhelmed by the scale of the problems.

WOW. HOW DO I EVEN START?

Yes, this may seem like a lot, especially when I throw in some galaxy-brain thinking about the nature of capitalism. But, not to worry: there are simple steps you can take to help you respond to the shifting nature of your customer base, the need to be authentic, and generally the desire to do well BY doing good, and this book is all about meeting you where you are in your process and giving you a place to start. Actually, you are probably doing some of these things. So, let's get to it.

There are three areas for you to consider: (1) how you make your money; (2) how you spend your money; and (3) how you invest in your people. This can be so simple that the steps you need to take can fit on one page—in fact, if you go to Table 1.1, Good Business Definitions, you'll see them all there!

This worksheet walks you through all you need to do to harness the power of equitable impact for your business. The first row focuses on how you make your money—what kind of products or services you offer, and generally how your business model helps align your profit creation with the creation of equitable impact. The second row concentrates on how you spend your money—both in terms of your inputs into your products and services, but also into ancillary things like your office supplies, benefits for employees, and even investment opportunities. The final row, "How you invest in your people," emphasizes aligning your company values with your company practices and seeing your employees as an asset to your company, not a commodity.

TABLE 1.1 Good Business Definitions

Good Business Components	Definition
How you make your money	Anything related to your core business model or how you generate revenue for your company. This includes operations and processes related to product development and production, services you offer to customers, or anything else that drives revenue.
How you spend your money	What your company spends money on in service of your core business model. This includes anything directly spent on creating a product or service, but also other indirect expenses for business operations.
How you invest in your people	Everything that goes into the hiring, training, and retention of your company's workforce. This includes intangible aspects of your workplace culture, but also direct investments in your talent—which could overlap with "How you spend your money."

The rows in Table 1.2, the Good Business Worksheet, represent the areas of focus, while the columns represent the steps to take to implement changes within each area. Each section has a "first step"—which is, not surprisingly, the first thing you need to do to make changes in your company. The other rows represent what I call the "Innovate-Accelerate-Decelerate" cycle, which is a continuous improvement process where you identify potential changes to your organization—either from outside or inside your company—and then apply them or ramp them up in your operations. You can also stop, or "decelerate," harmful activities that are not aligned with your values or the impact you want to create.

TABLE 1.2 Good Business Worksheet

How you make your money

First Step: Understand Your Business Model	Innovate	Accelerate	Decelerate

How you spend your money

First Step: Understand the Impact of Your Spend	Innovate	Accelerate	Decelerate

How you invest in your people

First Step: Understand Your Values Alignment	Innovate	Accelerate	Decelerate

In the next three chapters, I will walk you through each section, and help you determine what makes sense for how your company can integrate elements of equitable impact into its operations. Each chapter has its own iteration of the Good Business Worksheet; the worksheet in this chapter is actually a summary of those three worksheets, which you can complete on your own or with a team. Like Doc-Scan, this section may not be the best place for you (or your boss) to start. There may be more opportunities in the next chapters, or even the final chapter about the preconditions needed to execute on some of these tasks. Or, you may just need to spend time with the business case sections to understand better how your company fits into these global trends.

As you dig deeper into the Good Business Worksheet and the next three chapters, you'll learn that even though there are three parts to the worksheet, the process isn't linear. You may not be able to complete the full worksheet right now, but, if that is the case, focus your energies instead on spending or values alignment. As you go through the worksheet and read each chapter, you may find a section that doesn't resonate or is not the best place for you (or your boss) to start. If that happens, move on. There will be more opportunities in later sections or chapters—even the final chapter—about the preconditions needed to execute some of these things. You may want to concentrate on the business cases I present to understand better how your company fits into the global trends.

If you decide to implement the holy trinity of capitalism throughout your company, you will, at some point, have to complete all three elements of the worksheet. It will put you on a path to create an evolving, interlocking process that reinforces the "why" behind your Equitable Impact Venn diagram: the root cause of the problem you want to solve; the passion and values of your company; and the assets you bring through your business operations. Steps you take to complete the worksheet will help you refine how you think about equitable impact, and what you bring to tackling the problem you set out to solve. The steps build off one another and inform decisions across your company.

It's fine to complete the worksheets on your own, but the process of completing them will be more powerful if you do it as a team. Integrating equitable impact into your company is a huge undertaking, and will be easier if you bring along critical members of your organization. Engaging key members of staff in the initial conversation will help secure their buy-in and surface the best ideas from the start. To help with this, each chapter includes a sample discussion agenda. (They are also available online at CapEQimpact.com.)

If this isn't feasible or you are one of the few—or only—people in your company looking to harness equitable impact to help you do well BY doing good, the Good Business Worksheets can still help. They are designed as a simple way to illustrate the quick wins and opportunities for customer growth and revenue expansion. Doing them on your own can give you an important tool to help convince others to get on board with this shift in your operation. For example, you can just hand the worksheets to your boss or head of your department when you've completed them to clearly explain what you want to do and how you propose to do it. (For more on how to manage a change management process, check out Chapter 5 on the CapEQ™ continuum.)

You can start anywhere on the worksheet and in the chapters to come, but don't be surprised if you end up somewhere you didn't think you'd be. That's the beauty of this work—you start somewhere, and you end up everywhere.

Achieving Equitable Impact Through Your Business Model

I f you want to make an equitable impact that lasts, you will have to make certain that what you do is the "main course" of your business, and not a "side dish." This is critical because if it's merely a side dish, your customers will smell it, call out your BS, and you'll be seen as inauthentic and miss out on the benefits of doing well BY doing good.

What follows is a personal story to show the importance of authenticity. In my day job at CapEQ, I have the privilege of working with different types of entrepreneurs and businesses around the country who are trying to grow their businesses by "doing good." They bring me in to help them with anything from a talent management plan to market analysis to project implementation. Because the work I do is so different depending on the client, I always spend a lot of time getting to know the people I'm working for and understanding their unique needs. I pride myself on the recommendations I give, but, as you might expect, my recommendations don't always land right away.

THE ROLE OF AUTHENTICITY
ON SOCIAL IMPACT

Several years ago, I consulted with a company that had recently been acquired by a small private equity firm. I'll call it Doc-Scan. Doc-Scan was a midsized company with several hundred employees providing digital imaging services to corporations and government agencies. They work with clients to digitize their old paper files and also help them store those new digital files in a way that improves the client's business operations.

When the private equity firm invested in Doc-Scan, they were doing well, but needed a push in order to grow bigger and faster. They had been around for decades and their operations had stagnated. I did my due diligence and began to walk them through how I would help them shake up their work, attract new clients, and expand their operations.

I went through the three different sections of the Good Business Worksheet with Doc-Scan—how you make your money; how you spend your money; and how you invest in your people—but my recommendations and support focused primarily on how they made their money through their core service—document scanning.

To me, this was a no-brainer in terms of reorientating their work. Document scanning and digital information management cut down on paper, and therefore reduced unnecessary waste. If they positioned themselves as an environmentally-focused organization, Doc-Scan would be able to access a completely new market—companies looking to "go green"—and build on their decades of success to reach a new level of growth.

Well, let's just say this "green" recommendation fell pretty flat. My recommendation didn't fit their Equitable Impact Venn Diagram. It wasn't authentic. I was suggesting something focused on an environmental root cause, when they wanted to focus on changing their talent management practices to better invest in the well-being of their community.

As we worked through the different elements of the framework, they decided they wanted more support—with how to invest in your people (see Chapter 4), which ended up being a better fit for the company. This more authentic focus led to a better product at a better margin and also gave them access to new customers. After a few years, they received additional investment and further expanded their operations.

This example illustrates that regardless of what you do to engage with social issues, it must be authentic—the "main course" of your operations, not a side dish. If it's not, it can detract from what makes your business unique, and can cost you customers who know a marketing scam when they see one. Remember: two-thirds of consumers want to buy from companies that create social impact,[1] and authenticity is important to over 90 percent of consumers.[2] You cannot have social impact without the authenticity.

HOW TO ENSURE EQUITABLE IMPACT IS PRIORITY #1

This chapter and the two that follow walk you through one element of the Good Business Worksheet. Each begins with a "business case," which outlines trends around the world that highlight the need to focus on equitable and social impact within your core business operations. They then offer a "first step" process for how you can begin analyzing and changing your company's practices. Once the "first step" is complete, the Innovate-Accelerate-Decelerate cycle will help you determine what to consider for further action. There are also specific callouts and resources that will help you on your journey.

BUSINESS CASE: HOW YOU
MAKE YOUR MONEY

How you make your money is the most essential part of any business. Right? Your products and services are core to your operations, and it is there that you will find the most opportunity to embed social or environmental components.

But don't jump to conclusions too quickly. What you offer is only one side of the equation. On the other side of how you make your money are, of course, your customers—the people who buy your products and services. For this reason, today's demographic shifts and changes in consumer behavior make the strongest business case for why it makes sense for you to do well BY doing good.

The first big trend is the massive wealth transfer and increased purchasing power of the millennial generation (those born roughly between 1980 and 2000). They have surpassed boomers as America's largest generation,[3] and their spending is commensurate with their size. Their total purchasing power is $200 billion annually,[4] and it will only increase as they begin to inherit wealth from their parents. By some estimates, over $68 trillion will be transferred to the millennial generation by 2030.[5]

As I noted in Chapter 1, the millennial generation is much more socially conscious than previous generations, especially when it comes to their spending habits. They are much more likely to purchase a product from a company they see as "sustainable."[6] Almost 90 percent of millennials are willing to switch their purchasing decisions to support a company that is committed to a social cause,[7] and 42 percent say corporate responsibility is important to their purchasing decisions compared with just 35 percent of the general population.[8]

These trends are even more pronounced among millennial women. Consumer research from Merkle showed that more than 80 percent of millennial women said that a company's sustainability practices influenced their purchasing decision. Almost the same number said price was an influencing factor. They also found that millennial women make up the bulk of the purchasing power of their generation, about 85 percent of the total annual spending of the market.[9] Their influence and their focus on social issues will only continue to grow as they advance in their careers and take more ownership of their family's finances and spending habits.

The top five issues millennials care about, according to a Nielsen survey, are food and hunger, environmental sustainability, education, public health, and racial equality (see Figure 2.1). Again, don't jump to conclusions. As we now know, authenticity and values alignment are more important than simply "taking on a cause." As one respondent told Nielsen, "Brands should engage with issues related to the product. I don't care if a candy company cares about net neutrality, but a telecom company

Important for Brands to Address
Thinking about how brands engage with social issues, which of the following, if any, do you think are important for brands to address?
1. Food & Hunger ▲
2. Environmental Sustainability ▲
3. Education
4. Public Health ▲
5. Racial Equality
6. Poverty
7. Animal Welfare ▲
8. Water & Sanitation
9. Employee Satisfaction
10. Bullying

FIGURE 2.1 Top 10 issues important to millennials[12]

better be on the right side of the issue."[10] Their numbers back up this idea too: about 74 percent of survey respondents said they were more likely to buy from a company who cares about issues they care about, and a similar 70 percent said they were more likely to buy from a company that handles social issues well, no matter what the issue is.[11] This reinforces the idea that if you want to respond to the changing habits and desires of millennials, you've got to do the work to make sure the social causes you're engaging with are authentic and aligned with your business model.

(Note: Although the top issues on this list are food, the environment, and education, I have used examples from my own experience—education, workforce training, and racial equity. No matter the area, the process is the same, and you can apply the tools and resources to any issue.)

Another core feature of the millennial generation is that they are more diverse than earlier generations, racially and ethnically. A little over half of millennials are white, as compared to two-thirds of those 55+.[13] This means the growing millennial consumer market is going to look and behave significantly different from previous consumer groups. Perhaps as important, the research on changing demographics of the younger generations show this trend will continue, creating opportunities into the future.

Companies should be ready to respond to these demographic trends in the same way they are shaping their products and services based on shifting consumer preferences around social causes.

One obvious change that businesses can make is ensuring more diversity in the marketing of their products. Consumers won't want to buy your products if they don't see themselves in how you present what you are selling. This change is already happening across the industry, with more Black and brown people showing up in ads in all industries. However, surface-level changes are not enough. You have to go deeper and authentically engage in what your new and changing consumer market wants.

The two biggest groups of color within the millennial and post-millennial generation are Black and Hispanic/Latino. Digging into the consumer preferences of these groups, you'll find similar interest in and motivation around social issues and causes. Around 40 percent of Black adult consumers of all ages expect companies to support social causes; that is a higher percentage than the overall population.[14] Hispanics and Latinos—the largest and fastest growing demographic group— also think that engagement in community issues is important. Over 80 percent of Hispanics and Latinos say that if a company is more engaged with their community, they will be more likely to support that company. But only around 50 percent of Hispanics and Latinos say that their values are shared by major brands.[15] A Hispanic Sentiment Study found that Hispanics and Latinos overwhelmingly feel they are not sufficiently valued by companies. Over 80 percent of them say that they should be more valued by companies than they are today.[16] Authentically connecting with and engaging with this group can lead to increased loyalty and customer acquisition. (All of this data speaks to broad trends within groups, but of course, there are variations within groups: a young man of Puerto Rican descent living in New York may have different preferences than an older female Cuban immigrant living in Miami, just like a southern Black women in her sixties has different motivations than a teenage boy in the Midwest with mixed-race ancestry. The nuances of your brand message will have to depend on the specifics of your market.)

Both of these demographic groups represent massive untapped consumer purchasing potential. Nielsen research found that Black consumer choices are increasingly becoming mainstream products, and "investment in connecting with Black consumers can often yield sizable general market returns."[17] Nielsen gives the example of the health and beauty industry and its increasing recognition of the need for a range of products to meet the needs of Black consumers, which has created a multiplicity of products that appeal to both Black customers as well as the general population.

These demographic trends and shifting consumer preferences mean one thing for your business: you need to think differently about your products, services, and operations if you want to attract and retain customers and employees, and the biggest and best way you can do that is to think through how your business model is aligned with equitable impact.

THE EFFECT OF HISTORIC DISCRIMINATION ON MARKETING TO COMMUNITIES OF COLOR

There's been an active and negative interpretation of what's possible from investments in people and communities of color. Stereotypes remain about what groups are seen as "risky" investments and which are not. It is is true that Black and brown communities have significantly less wealth and purchasing power than white people, as a result of generations of underinvestment and outright discrimination against people of color.

Policies like redlining limited people of color from buying property in desirable neighborhoods. Japanese internment during World War II literally ripped apart communities and the wealth and investments that were being built there. Historical and persistent employment discrimination has prevented people of color from advancing in all major industries. All of these trends have led to an ongoing income and wealth gap between white people and people of color. In 2016, the wealth of the average white family was over $700,000 higher than the average Black or Hispanic family. This means the average white family had five times the wealth of the average Hispanic family, and seven times that of the average Black family. Gaps in income are similar: the average white man will earn over $2.7 million in his lifetime compared to $1.8 million for the average Black man and $2 million for the average Hispanic man.[18]

What this means for business is that the economic growth of our country is limited for everyone; we're all leaving money on the table. The W.K. Kellogg Foundation found that if all racial gaps were closed by 2050, we could add $8 trillion to the economy.[19] Similarly, if businesses owned by Black people had the capacity to hire the same number of employees as white businesses, there would be an additional $55 billion in the economy.[20]

FIRST STEP: UNDERSTAND YOUR BUSINESS MODEL

Once you acknowledge that *how* you make your money can improve your customers' trust and engagement with your business, the first step is to look at your business model to see how you can better leverage it for equitable impact. For some companies, this requires actually *understanding* their business model for the first time.

As a current business leader, future business leader, or someone who works closely for one, it may seem silly for me to ask you to take time to better understand your business model. I can hear you now, "Of course, I understand my business! I commit my blood, sweat, and tears to it every single day!! Don't tell me I don't know what I'm doing!"

Well, that is definitely true, but sometimes it's important to take a step back from your day-to-day work to examine the bigger picture: what you are doing, why you are doing it, and how you are doing it. These kinds of strategic planning conversations are frequent in successful, long-term businesses. A good way to ensure equitable impact becomes your business's main course is to integrate questions about how and why you are

creating equitable impact throughout your core business operations. Given the work and focus of your company, what could
your unique role be in creating equitable impact? Remember
the young Nielsen survey respondent's comment: "I don't care
if a candy company cares about net neutrality, but a telecom
company better be on the right side of the issue." What's your
version of net neutrality? What issue is so core to your operations that you better be on the right side of it?

The Equitable Impact Venn Diagram (Figure 1.2) can help
you determine your core business purpose. What is authentic
to your company that you do that no one else does? What sits
at the intersection of the problem you are trying to solve, your
company's values and passion, and the assets contained within
your company? These are the bigger picture questions that can
help you see your company in a different way.

Let's revisit Doc-Scan, which we examined earlier. I was
brought in during a period of transition; the company had
recently been acquired and the new owners were looking for
changes that would increase profitability and growth. Doc-Scan
had been operating in a certain way for decades, and I helped
them walk through all aspects of their business model and
operations, from how they hired their employees, to how they
worked with clients, to how they sold themselves in the market.

Using the Equitable Impact Venn Diagram, I helped Doc-
Scan come to understand their unique role in creating equitable
impact. They believed that accessing information can unlock
innovation and progress, leading to more innovative companies, thriving economies, and sustainable communities. Once
they defined this as their core purpose, it allowed them to look
at their business model differently: they saw their company
could better support their employees and, by extension, build
stronger and more prosperous communities (more on how they
did this in Chapter 4).

This repositioning helped them stand out from their competitors in the paper scanning industry, which is frequently a

competitive "race to the bottom" industry where companies compete against each other to have the lowest price-per-page-scanned cost. Their understanding of purpose helped them stand out with clients, particularly government agencies, who were able to partner with Doc-Scan as a way to invest in a community's residents, and even allowed them to charge a premium for their services.

This example shows how, in the real world, these components are interrelated. Rethinking your business model may lead you to change your company's hiring policies. Steps discussed in future chapters may make you want to come back to this section and answer some questions differently. That's because a company truly operating at the highest level will have all of their business components aligned and committed to equitable impact.

Every company can tap into the good business of equitable impact, just as Doc-Scan did. In the rest of the chapter, I will walk you through the steps of how to do so.

HOW TO CREATE IMPACT USING YOUR BUSINESS MODEL

There are many great resources out there to help you understand your core business model and leverage it for increased growth and customer acquisition. Books like *Good to Great*, by Jim Collins, *Switch: How to Change When Change Is Hard*, by the Heath Brothers, and *To Sell Is Human*, by Daniel Pink are just some of the many great resources to help with strategic planning and creating a solid business model poised for growth.

Once you take that first step in identifying how your core business model can be leveraged for equitable impact, there are a few areas you can consider to help you shift your core business operations.

Acquisition

There's nothing like buying another company to help shift or expand your business model. The work has already been done for you! All you have to do is sign the check.

OK, OK . . . it's not that simple, and of course I know most companies are not big enough to buy a company that adds another product line to their business or helps them expand into other markets. But, if you are at that level and can consider acquisitions as a way to diversify your business operations, are you thinking about equitable impact when you have those conversations? In the same way you would consider acquiring a company for their strong track record in customer service and then applying its impact across your company, you would consider acquiring a company with strong evidence of equitable impact and then applying its effect on other areas within your company.

In fact, if you are looking to acquire a company for any reason, make sure that you screen them for aspects of equitable impact; do your due diligence just as you would on other aspects of the company's operations. Does the company value the same things you do? Is the company actively doing harm on social issues in some way? Will it be as committed to your equitable impact processes as your existing team?

Product or Service Innovation

Acquisition is not the only way companies can adapt or change what they are doing, of course. Most of the time, these business model shifts come internally—Apple didn't start out making cell phones, after all. You hire good people to work at your company, and they are probably just as aware of the social impact trends as you are. Bring together a team of people to think about how equitable impact can be better integrated within your existing products or services, as well as new ideas for revenue streams that can be developed that both solve problems and increase profits. This is a great project to assign to younger employees looking to make their mark on the company, because, in keeping with their demographic tendencies, the younger generations are more interested in social impact and doing work that aligns with their values.

With an internal social innovation team in place, you can think through how to change your existing products or services as well as new products you may develop. Maybe you can go greener with your supply chain (more on that in Chapter 3), or develop a partnership with a nonprofit through a service you offer. Anything that your company creates or does has an impact, and so considering how that impact could be more positive for society or the environment will only help strengthen your connection with your customers.

Customer Engagement

Finally, also consider how you are directly connecting with customers and creating an "experience" for them. The ubiquity of social media has made it easier to connect directly with customers and create a community around your products or your brand. Businesses frequently leverage these communities to help sell their products, but what about achieving some equitable impact goals? Maybe you can leverage them for a fundraising drive for a cause, or coordinate a call-to-action campaign around an important bill or policy that aligns with your business operations. While it may not be directly related to your business model, these kinds of asks can increase engagement with your customers and strengthen their identity as a member of the community you are creating around your business.

Later in the chapter, you'll find Table 2.2, an expanded version of the Good Business Worksheet focused on "how you make your money," which includes these questions and will help you apply the lessons discussed in this chapter. If you are doing this exercise yourself, you can answer the questions right on the page (you can find a downloadable and editable version at CapEQimpact.com). If you are doing this as a group, you'll also find a facilitation guide online there. I usually do these exercises with the leadership team of a company, and recommend doing this with a team of at least three people from across the organization.

The next section will help you go deeper into each of these three areas of impact—Acquisition, Product or Service Innovation, and Customer Engagement—and illustrate how you can use them to integrate changes across your company. As you go through the steps of the Good Business Worksheet, remember to think about what's authentic to your business. Some proposed changes may not sit right with you because they are outside of the core scope of your business model; for example, if you are a catering company, you may want to stick to food-related innovations and not try to acquire a company that sells jewelry from artisans in sub-Saharan Africa. Doc-Scan could have gone with an environmental focus, but it didn't seem like the right fit for the team at the time, and it wouldn't have been authentic to their company. Don't be afraid to push yourself to think differently, but also don't push yourself so far that you are uncomfortable with where you land, or it takes you away from what makes your business unique. This is a delicate dance, but in the rest of the chapter I will take you through the right steps.

THE INNOVATE-ACCELERATE-DECELERATE CYCLE TO LEVERAGE MAKING MONEY

Once you have explored the different areas of impact within your core business model and what they mean for your company's alignment with equitable impact, it's time to move into what I call the "Innovate-Accelerate-Decelerate" cycle, which is a repetitive process of analyzing your company's operations and determining what you can double down on and what you can change to make equitable impact a core part of your operations and offering to your customers. It involves innovating on your existing processes to bring in or develop new ideas, accelerating the good work you are already doing, and reducing or removing the aspects of your business that are doing harm.

TABLE 2.1 Innovate-Accelerate-Decelerate defined

Good Business Components	Definition
Innovate	Creating or importing something new to your company that leads to equitable impact
Accelerate	Building and growing something within your company that's already creating equitable impact
Decelerate	Stopping something that's causing harm and is counter to your equitable impact goals

Innovate

The first component is "innovate," by which I mean, consider what changes you can make to your company to increase your ability to solve social problems. Often this could be importing a leading edge from your industry that can drive impact or developing an idea of your own based on your company's unique value proposition to customers and communities.

Innovate Through Acquisition: As I mentioned earlier, acquisition is a great way to innovate for equitable impact, and a great example of a company importing innovation is Gap's acquisition of Athleta in 2008. Athleta is a women's apparel company that has made strong external commitments to both women's empowerment and sustainability efforts—and, at the time they were acquired, they were on the cutting edge of the industry in terms of their commitment to social causes. Athleta makes its social impact goals public on its website, and revises them as they achieve them (or don't) to hold themselves accountable.

They have committed, for example, that 80 percent of their materials would be made with sustainable fibers, and 25 percent of their products would be made using water-saving techniques.[21] Because of their commitment to making a social impact, in 2018 they received B Corp Certification, which requires an intensive process that sets standards for social impact in business.[22] Athleta is one the largest apparel brands to receive this distinction.

Athleta is Gap's fastest growing brand.[23] Acquiring it has helped the company commit more to social causes and integrate social impact across all of its affiliates. (In 2019, it committed to using 100 percent sustainable cotton in all of its brands by 2025.[24]) I worked with Athleta to help them diversify and expand their customer base beyond predominantly white women to allow them to fully realize their corporate brand promise of empowering all women.

Acquisition is a great way for companies to bring in innovation and learn from that experience, but it isn't always possible. (Not everyone can make a $150 million investment like Gap did to buy Athleta![25]) Sometimes you have to create innovation within your company to be able to leverage the full potential of your business.

Innovate from Within: Another way to innovate on a business model, as I said earlier, is to do it internally. When I worked at GE during the early days of the internet, internet startups were seen as a big threat to GE's bottom line. Instead of going the acquisition route, which was certainly available to a large company like GE, management decided to create our own innovation team within the company to develop our own, internal internet startup. Because of my computer science background, I was brought in to help that team as an e-business analyst (back then, we put "e"s in front of everything). We ended up creating the cheekily named DestroyYourBusiness.com, which helped GE conduct transportation logistics via an internet web platform. In fact, doing this successfully helped GE understand the positive innovation the internet was and apply it across all of its other business areas.

Accelerate

Chances are you are already doing something that aligns your corporate values with equitable impact. Whether that's an employee volunteer day or a donation of some of your profits to a cause, most businesses already include some element of social engagement in their company. The problem is that they are frequently a "one-off" or to the side of core operations—the side dish not the "main course."

If that is the case in your company, take those elements that already exist and accelerate them within and across your company. For example, if you are looking to connect with customers and tackle social problems, why not begin with what you are already doing? It can be easier to start with something that is already in place, no matter how small, than to start from scratch and spin in circles to determine the best ways to proceed.

Let's say you have a charitable giving program. A lot of companies donate to local nonprofits or community-based organizations to be good stewards in the places they operate. If you have a charitable giving program in place, take a look at it and think about how you can make it a core component of your business model. You may want to pick charities that are aligned with your products and services—such as women's empowerment if you are a beauty brand—and incorporate a charitable incentive for customers when they purchase your products, such as donating a certain amount of your profits on each item sold.

This "embedded donation" model has become a standard mode of operations for recent startups and more established companies. Companies like TOMS Shoes and Warby Parker have a "buy one, give one" model in which they give away one product for each one sold (a pair of shoes in the case of TOMS and glasses for Warby Parker). These companies (and many others) were founded with this model in mind, and have always seen their purpose as both delivering quality products to customers and giving back to communities who need it.

This kind of "buy one, give one" model, or the similar "we'll give X percentage of our profits to charity," is typically easy for a company to start doing, but it is usually just a first step. Some companies, including TOMS, which is probably the most well-known company using this model, have been criticized for actually harming the communities they support by sending free shoes to developing countries, rather than investing in those communities by creating good jobs by manufacturing the shoes in those countries, which could provide more economic empowerment and long-term sustainability.

Commitments to donate to nonprofits are sometimes seen as pandering or less-than-authentic steps, particularly for those companies that have a history of bad corporate practices. Taking on these types of business practices isn't inherently a bad thing, as it can create a strong bond with customers and provide a powerful signal about your values in a way that advertising can't. But like all the advice I present, it needs to be done in ways that are both authentic to your company and actually create a real, tangible impact.

Cotopaxi, a company that develops sustainable outdoor products, is an example of a company that takes the idea of giving and accelerates it through its organizational operations. Cotopaxi is an outdoor apparel and gear company that was started by Davis Smith, who started several successful e-commerce businesses before he decided to create a company that would pair fighting poverty with the sale of products. Not only does Cotopaxi, which, like Athleta, is a B Corporation, give 1 percent of its profits to fighting poverty, it also ensures that its supply chain meets the highest ethical standards. It partners with factories to set expectations around worker safety and labor practices as well as to incorporate "remnant fabrics" that would otherwise be discarded in its products. It has also received Climate Neutral certification, which means it operates with a 100 percent carbon-neutral footprint.[26]

I don't bring up Cotopaxi to suggest that your business should reach that level of equitable impact right away. These types of operational commitments take a lot of time and energy, and require thoughtful planning. But Cotopaxi illustrates what is possible when impact is the main course and not just a side dish.

As you think about what to accelerate to help incorporate equitable impact into your business model, consider the concept of community building as a different way to think about customer engagement. Community building (sometimes called network building or simply "brand ambassadors") is becoming a more common practice as social media takes on greater importance as a marketing or communications strategy. Community building is when you intentionally allow your customers to engage with and define your brand for you, and become "ambassadors" for your products and services. This limits some of your ability to define your products and services, but it makes your outreach and engagement with your customers so much more authentic because they themselves are defining what your business means to them.

Athleta has a brand ambassador program that helps spread the message of their work and connect with other customers. Called "FitPros," they use female fitness instructors and other health and wellness professionals who are part of a community of people who love and use Athleta products and are also committed to women's empowerment.

In another life, I was a FitPro myself and gave Athleta some shout-outs during my classes. Athleta has been able to create an enthusiastic and loyal customer base because they identify with its social cause and its authenticity commitment to it, which is why ambassadors like me spread Athleta's message, products, and services like a parent sharing videos of their kids in the school play.

Decelerate

Now we get to the hardest part. Deceleration is when you have to take a long, hard look at what your company is doing with and think about what you should stop doing to be more aligned with your values and your customers' values.

If you are reading this book, you've probably started this process, or at least have some ideas about what company practices you think should change. If you are the boss, they may be within your power to change. If you aren't the boss, raising ideas that require your company to step on the brakes a bit could be very challenging and take a lot of personal political capital. My hope is that what you've read so far gives you the tools to make the case for why stopping bad practices needs to happen sooner rather than later if your company wants to remain competitive going forward. There are so many examples of companies changing the way they do business, either because of customer pressure, employee pressure, or a combination of both. As globalization and corporate consolidation become more and more common, the impact of companies, good and bad, has become clearer. Consider the beverage giants Coca-Cola and PepsiCo. Both of these companies' flagship beverages have been around for over a century. They are among the most recognizable brands around the world. Their operations are massive, and use up a massive amount of water too. Leaders of both companies have recognized that they need to have good water practices to remain competitive. Neither has set out to be a sustainable environmental company, but because of how they operate, they needed to make that shift. Coca-Cola has set a 2030 water security strategy and, so far, has replenished 1.75 trillion liters of water.[27] PepsiCo has improved its water use efficiency by 15 percent and delivered safe water access to 55 million people.[28]

If you are a small- or medium-sized business, large shifts like these may not be feasible, but there are smaller changes you can make to your business model that are easier and will even save you money. Maybe you have a wasteful supply chain. Spending time eliminating that waste could reduce your costs. Maybe your labor practices aren't great. Increasing employee benefits could improve the livelihoods of your employees and also reduce turnover (more on that in Chapter 4).

Again, pointing out the things that need to change isn't an easy task—even if you are the boss. The tools and resources included here can help you make these conversations clearer and easier. The next section will walk you through how to put this all together.

PUT IT ALL TOGETHER AND CHANGE HOW YOUR COMPANY MAKES MONEY

We'll use the Good Business Worksheet to put all these elements together and see what these changes mean for your company. Table 2.2 is another iteration of the Good Business Worksheet. It is designed to help you dive into your business model and how you make your money. Once you work through this worksheet, summarize what you came up with or agreed to with your team on the sheet—which you can download at CapEQimpact.com. As with each chapter, you will also find a Good Business Agenda (Table 2.3) to help you and your team walk through completing this iteration of the worksheet.

This worksheet has two essential purposes: identifying (1) the areas of impact within your company and (2) the opportunities that exist within those areas. You begin by understanding your company's business model. Once you've done this, the Innovate-Accelerate-Decelerate cycle guides you through implementing these changes. Each iteration of the worksheet at each step of the Innovate-Accelerate-Decelerate cycle also includes a standard question—*Will these changes affect certain groups more than others and will they worsen or ignore disparities?*—adapted

TABLE 2.2 Good Business Worksheet, Part 1: How you make your money

How you make your money

First Step: Understand Your Business Model	Innovate	Accelerate	Decelerate
Which areas of impact can help align your business model with equitable impact? • Acquisition • Product/Service Innovation • Customer Engagement	*Which areas of impact within your company can benefit from innovation?*	*Which areas of impact can benefit from an acceleration of impact practices?*	*Which areas of impact in your company are doing more harm than good?*
	How will you bring innovative practices into these areas of impact?	*How will you accelerate impact practices within these areas of impact?*	*What changes can you make in these areas of impact to decelerate the harm being done?*
What low-hanging fruit that would be easy to change can you identify?	*What are your next steps toward implementing these changes across your company?*	*What are your next steps toward implementing these changes across your company?*	*What are your next steps toward implementing these changes across your company?*
What higher-impact areas can you identify?	*Will these changes affect certain groups more than others, and will they worsen or ignore disparities?*	*Will these changes affect certain groups more than others, and will they worsen or ignore disparities?*	*Will these changes affect certain groups more than others, and will they worsen or ignore disparities?*

TABLE 2.3 Good Business Agenda: How you make your money

Time	Topic	Guiding Questions
5 minutes	**Business model alignment**	*How would you describe the company's core business model? Is there any disagreement?* Note: This part of the conversation should be quick. If it's not, you may need to have another meeting!
10 minutes	**Areas of impact**	*In which areas of impact are there opportunities to help better align the company's business model with equitable impact?* Choose all that are relevant: • Acquisition • Product/Service Innovation • Customer Engagement
15 minutes	**Low-hanging fruit and high impact actions**	*What are some opportunities that your company can easily change in these areas of impact that will give it quick wins on equitable impact?* *What opportunities will require more time and resources, but will have higher mpact long-term?*
25 minutes	**Implementation plan: The Innovate-Accelerate-Decelerate Cycle**	Develop a plan of action by answering the following questions: • *How will you bring innovative practices into these areas of impact?* • *Which areas of impact can benefit from an acceleration of impact practices?* • *Which areas of impact within your company are doing more harm than good?* • *Will these changes affect certain groups more than others, and will they worsen or ignore disparities?*
5 minutes	**Next steps**	*What are your next steps to implementing these changes across your company?*

from a tool used by the Race Matters Institute, to help you consider diversity, equity and inclusion (DEI) throughout this process. As you make decisions for equitable impact, it's important to consider what blind spots you may have and who isn't included in your decision-making process that might need to be. By integrating this into each step of the Good Business Worksheet you can ensure you are not replicating inequitable processes and policies that may be in your company. I tell my clients this makes DEI "built in, not bolted on."

The worksheet in this chapter focuses on "How you make your money"; the next two chapters contain their own versions of the worksheet. Once you complete them all, I recommend you go back to Chapter 1 and complete the full worksheet overview.

When to Consider How to Make Your Money

Although taking the steps in the Good Business Worksheet can be done at any time, there are circumstances when taking certain steps will be easier and have greater impact. Considering questions around "how to make your money" is best done when you are undertaking a strategic planning process or beginning a new product or service line. Ensuring that impact is the main course of your business model means you have to plan for that as early as possible so the sooner you explore these questions, the better. If you are just starting your company—that's great! These questions can help you create a business plan that infuses equitable impact. If your company is up and running, no problem: the next time you have a far-reaching strategic conversation, bring this part of the Good Business Worksheet to that meeting.

Steps to Completing the Good Business Worksheet

Let's go through the steps:

Step 1: Understand your core business model. This should be pretty simple, as most people in the company should understand the products or services you offer as well as your unique market niche. But don't assume this; begin the meeting with a discussion of what people think your business model is and why.

Step 2: Consider what changes to make once there's agreement or understanding about your core business model based on the following areas of impact:

- Acquisition
- Product or Service Innovation
- Customer Engagement

You don't necessarily need ideas for each area of impact; in fact, you probably shouldn't, because that means you aren't focusing enough on what is authentic to your company and you could spread yourself too thin. You want to focus on what makes sense for your company. Acquisition may not be an option for you, but redesigning a product line might. This worksheet isn't about checking each box, but actually for determining what makes sense for your company for equitable impact integration. Once you have chosen your top areas for impact, circle them on the worksheet. Make sure you do this! Physically interacting with the worksheet is a way to ensure everyone is on the same page, since it'll literally be written in black and white.

Step 3: Go deeper into each area's potential once you know its impact. The first thing to consider are the low-hanging fruit opportunities. These are things that are easy to do and can be thought of as quick wins to show the value of equitable impact on your business. It could be something like setting up a campaign for your customers focused on a social cause they care about, or buying carbon credits to offset the environmental impact of your supply chain. Once you figure out all your quick wins, write these opportunities down underneath the low-hanging fruit question.

This isn't just about easy fixes, though, so you also should think about the longer-term options that will take more resources but have a higher impact on your company and society. This may be an acquisition opportunity or the development of a new product line. Don't be afraid to think big and bold for these. Once you've got your ideas, write them under the high impact question in the first column.

Step 4: Implement these changes using the Innovate-Accelerate-Decelerate cycle once you have your ideas and opportunities nailed down. Start with innovate and determine which areas of impact you've selected could benefit from innovation, either from outside your company or by encouraging it from within. You could start a cross-functional, social-impact-focused innovation team to take a look at all your product or service offerings. These could be related to your answers to the low-hanging fruit or high impact question, or something else you want to consider.

Once you have the areas of impact that can benefit from innovation, write them down on the worksheet. Then, answer these questions to help with implementation and next steps:

- *How will you bring innovative practices into these areas of impact?* Another way to think about this question is: What innovative practices would be a good fit for your company and your team?
- *What are the next steps to implementing these changes across your company?* To put it another way, What needs to get done to allow these changes to happen? *Will these changes affect certain groups more than others, and will they worsen or ignore disparities?* You may recall, this is the standard DEI question referenced earlier. Another way to think about it is: What blind spots might you have as you think about implementing innovative ideas?

Write your answers down on the worksheet, and move on to the Accelerate column.

Step 5: Consider how you could accelerate good things already happening to support the opportunities within the areas of impact you've identified. Write down which areas of impact you think would benefit from this acceleration in the Accelerate column. Remember, acceleration can be things happening *within* your company as well as good work happening *outside* your company. You may have a competitor or partner that has established a social impact initiative, and you can join them in that. Answering the following questions can help you create your implementation plan:

- *How will you accelerate impact practices within these areas of impact?* Or: What is already going on that you can support and encourage?
- *What are the next steps you have to take to implement these changes across your company?* Or: How can you support team members to implement these acceleration strategies?
- *Will these changes affect certain groups more than others, and will they worsen or ignore disparities?* Or: Is there a group of people who isn't represented in this decision-making process who should be consulted on this change?

Step 6: Think about the harm your company may be doing, and how to decelerate those practices. Then, answer these questions to formulate your plan of action:

- *What changes can you make in these areas of impact to decelerate the harm being done?* Or: What can you stop doing that would help strengthen your core business model or operations?
- *What are your next steps to implementing these changes across your company?* Or: What steps do you need to take to stop these practices from continuing?
- *Will these changes affect certain groups more than others, and will they worsen or ignore disparities?* Or: Who has

been most harmed by these practices, and how can they be empowered?

Step 7: Make sure the team agrees on your answers to this section of the Good Business Worksheet. Then distribute it to those you think need to understand what you plan to do and why. You may want to post it in your workspace. Then, get to work and move on to the next part of the worksheet—"how you spend your money"—which I'll cover in the next chapter.

As you go through the different iterations of the worksheet, you'll probably find that some of the steps are similar or that your answers overlap. That's OK; that's how it should be. The Good Business Worksheet is intended to be a way to ground the process of integrating equitable impact into your company's operations; it is not meant to be a strictly rigid process. Sometimes, it's going to be more of an art than a science. My intention is to provide you with the tools and resources to help you through the process of changing how you do business to help you better prepare for the shifting demands of your customers and the changing nature of our economy. The process is iterative; for this reason, you should revisit your answers to these questions every so often. There may be new things you want to accelerate within your company, or something you realize you need to decelerate as soon as possible. The steps provided in the Good Business Worksheet are not fundamentally different from a typical continuous improvement process—I'm just suggesting additional questions to help you think through how to improve and measure your equitable impact alongside your normal business performance metrics.

Spotlight On: Racial Equity Underwriting[29]

Racial equity underwriting is an innovative process related to how certain companies make their money. Most companies or investors have a pretty strict process for how they determine who should receive loans or investments, and that process of taking on the risk of a loan or investment for some return is called "underwriting." Usually, the process includes a review of outstanding debt, credit scores, and the total value of the firm's assets—its inventory, for example, or someone's house.

If you've ever gotten a mortgage or purchased insurance, you've experienced this process. The underwriting process is a big part of how banks and other financial institutions make their money. However, as it's designed now, it is inherently biased toward helping those who already have wealth and other financial opportunities because the underwriting process relies on standardized indicators of "creditworthiness."

For this reason, traditional underwriting discriminates against people of color, because it relies on things like the value of a home to determine the creditworthiness of a potential borrower. Because of the ongoing segregation in this country and historical factors like redlining, people of color have lower homeownership rates. When they do own homes, they are valued less than a similar home would be in a "white" neighborhood. This discrimination prevents people of color from accruing wealth over time, and limits their ability to secure loans and other investments.

Many people and organizations in the industry today are revisiting the traditional approach to underwriting and working to develop a process that is more racially equitable and inclusive of everyone who needs a loan or investment. Beneficial State Foundation is a shareholder in Beneficial State Bank, a community development bank that is completely owned by nonprofit organizations; its profits are redistributed directly into communities. It recently launched Underwriting for Racial Justice, a national collaborative working to change underwriting practices to remove barriers to capital and support racial justice. In addition to being a shareholder in Beneficial State Bank, Beneficial State Foundation advocates for an equitable regulatory and policy agenda in banking, along with additional field-building activities to strengthen and connect different players involved in equitable banking.[30]

HOW YOU MAKE YOUR MONEY: SYDNEY'S JEWELRY SHOP

My seven-year-old daughter, Sydney, loves jewelry.

Her love of jewelry started very young, and as she got older, she was more and more interested in making her own. My husband and I bought her different jewelry-making kits, but she ignored them because she thought the materials in the kits were too constraining. Instead, she makes jewelry out of anything she can find. We now have set her up with a big box of art supplies that she can add to and take from whatever she needs. Her latest creations were bracelets that she likes to put on before she uses her Taekwondo moves on our other child, Dylan. She likes the warrior princess vibe they bring when she is charging into Dylan's room without permission.

She likes to make pieces for her family and friends, and while she hasn't quite gotten into selling them just yet, she might one day. I figured a potential jewelry-making business might be a helpful example to run through the Good Business Worksheet to illustrate what it might look like for any company.

Let's spend some time with Sydney to see how she would use these steps to change how she made her money to embed equitable impact across her business. (To be clear, this is hypothetical; no, I did not make my child actually do this!) You can see her final result in Table 2.4.

Step 1: She first thinks through her core business model. This is pretty easy since it is a straightforward business. She makes jewelry using the materials she has purchased and sells them for a little bit more than what she bought the materials for. She uses the revenue to buy more materials.

Step 2: Looking at the three areas of impact for how she makes her money, she isn't big enough (yet!) to acquire another company or product line, but she thinks she can make an impact in the other two areas.

Step 3: With a focus on product innovation and customer engagement, she considers what low-hanging fruit she can tackle first. Sydney decides she wants to form a partnership with a nonprofit because girls' empowerment is very important to her. An easy thing she can do is donate a part of her proceeds to a local nonprofit that helps girls learn how to code. Doing this helps create a bond with customers who care about this issue and increases their loyalty to her product. She knows this kind of "percent of profits donated" model is a pretty low bar for impact, so she also wants to think about the environmental impact of her product and how to reach the point where she has a carbon-neutral product.

Step 4: In terms of the Innovate-Accelerate-Decelerate cycle, she decides to innovate with her low-hanging fruit idea and partner with the nonprofit and create a bigger relationship than one focused solely on donations. In addition to donating part of her profits, she decides to give free pieces of jewelry to the girls in the program. The girls wear the jewelry at all their coding competitions, expanding her customer base and giving her access to those girls' networks as well as those of their parents.

For accelerate, she follows the Athleta example and sets up a community of those who believe in girls' empowerment and girls in STEM around her jewelry. She has a group of friends who love her jewelry, and leans into that and builds on the excitement that's already there. They are able to support the work of the nonprofit, and also connect with each other around the jewelry, make specific requests, and tell their friends about Sydney's product.

For decelerate, Sydney wants to use less and ultimately stop using environmentally unfriendly materials by creating a supply chain that has a better environmental impact. She knows that this may be hard to accomplish, but it's a long-term goal and something that's important to her product and her brand.

At each step of the Innovate-Accelerate-Decelerate cycle, she thinks through her blind spots and considers what she may be missing. Under innovate, she considers that the nonprofit she partners with may not actually be reaching the girls who are most in need, and decides to ask her point of contact how the organization can expand its outreach. For accelerate, she considers that by relying only on her friends, she may exclude some people who want to participate, so she puts up fliers to recruit others to join the group. As to decelerate, she considers that some smaller suppliers may not have a big presence online, so she considers expanding her research beyond the internet.

Table 2.4 is Sydney's completed "How you make your money" worksheet. Once she's done with this, she hangs it up over her jewelry-making table and gets ready to focus on part 2: How she spends her money!

TABLE 2.4 Good Business Worksheet, Part 1: How Sydney's jewelry shop makes its money

How you make your money

First Step: Understand Your Business Model	Innovate	Accelerate	Decelerate
Which areas of impact can help align your business model with equitable impact? • Product Innovation • Customer Engagement *What low-hanging fruit that would be easy to change can you identify?* • Donate a portion of profits to girls' empowerment nonprofit. *What higher impact areas can you identify?* • Create a carbon-neutral product.	*Which areas of impact within your company can benefit from innovation?* • Product Innovation *How will you bring innovative practices into these areas of impact?* • Create a partnership with a nonprofit to give free jewelry to participants in addition to donations. *What are your next steps toward implementing these changes across your company?* • Meet with nonprofit representative to propose partnership. *Will these changes affect certain groups more than others, and will they worsen or ignore disparities?* • Nonprofit may not work with those most in need—work to expand their outreach.	*Which areas of impact can benefit from an acceleration of impact practices?* • Customer Engagement *How will you accelerate impact practices within these areas of impact?* • Create community of customers interested in girls' empowerment and STEM. *What are your next steps toward implementing these changes across your company?* • Create first group of customers among closest friends. *Will these changes affect certain groups more than others, and will they worsen or ignore disparities?* • Advertise group to include people beyond friends.	*Which areas of impact in your company are doing more harm than good?* • Product Innovation *What changes can you make in these areas of impact to decelerate the harm being done?* • Work to create a carbon-neutral product. *What are your next steps toward implementing these changes across your company?* • Research environmentally friendly suppliers. *Will these changes affect certain groups more than others, and will they worsen or ignore disparities?* • Don't just rely on internet for research—also ask for recommendations from network.

ADDITIONAL RESOURCES
Equitable Impact: A Blueprint for Racial Equity

Lately, conversations about social impact and corporate social responsibility are broadening to include a discussion about race and racial equity. Many companies are not only mindful of their social impact, but also how they are talking about race, diversifying their workforce, and considering how their practices have an effect on people of color—positive or negative. This is driven by consumer trends similar to others I've discussed: 75 to 80 percent of Americans believe that companies should not only condemn structural racism, racial injustice, and police violence, but that they should take steps to create a more equitable future.[31]

The Good Business Worksheet and ideas presented in later chapters are designed to help you pull all the levers in your company to create equitable impact. Deciding how success in your company should be defined can be hard, but if you want to go deeper into what successful development of equitable impact could look like, I recommend using the CEO Blueprint for Racial Equity, developed by PolicyLink, FSG, and JUST Capital in partnership with CapEQ, which has also helped organizations operationalize the tool and embed it in our approach.

The blueprint advises CEOs who are attempting to integrate racial equity across their company and want to consider their company's influence on communities of color in their decision-making. The blueprint recommends that CEOs consider company impact in three areas:

1. Inside the company
2. Within the communities where the companies are headquartered and conduct business
3. At the broader societal level[32]

Many of their recommendations in these three areas align with recommendations in this book:

- Developing equitable HR practices

- Considering racial outcomes of the products they create
- Working with partners on policy changes

There is a companion resource to the blueprint that highlights how CEOs have used the recommendations and shares their insights.[33] You can find both resources at PolicyLink.org.

Racial Equity Investing

Investors have a huge influence on how our economy operates, which should require them to take an even more nuanced approach to creating equitable impact through how they make their money. Racial equity has taken on more salience and importance for investors in the last several years. Persistent racial gaps in income and wealth have been increasingly recognized as an emerging threat to economic growth and social resilience, and shocking events like the murder of George Floyd and other Black men and women by police, along with the disproportionate effect of the COVID-19 pandemic on communities of color, have forced investors to become more interested in racial equity practices when making investment decisions.

Investors are now looking to integrate a racial equity lens into their investing strategies to both increase their ability to close racial gaps within their own organizations and within the businesses and communities they invest in.

To support these efforts and encourage standardization in racial equity investment strategies, the Global Impact Investing Network (GIIN), in partnership with CapEQ and PolicyLink, a research and action institute, created a framework for racially equitable investing. This framework has three strategic goals:

1. Increasing the power of historically marginalized populations due to race and/or ethnicity
2. Shifting the perception of riskiness of investing in those populations
3. Creating just systems that produce equitable outcomes

We shorthanded these goals as "power, risk, and justice." Within each of these goals, investors can take a number of investment approaches to increase racially equitable outcomes:

Power: Shifting power through investing requires address- ing racial bias and ensuring equitable representation and decision-making within both investment firms and investee companies. Investments should aim to change the makeup of existing decision makers around capital allocation and imple- ment racially equitable policies to promote and increase the deployment of capital to businesses owned by and employed by marginalized populations disadvantaged as the result of race and/or ethnicity.

Risk: Creating equitable deal sourcing, due diligence, and terms can shift perceptions of risk. Investments should aim to change the concept of what are "risky" investments to allow more capital to flow to businesses and communities of historically marginalized populations due to race and/or ethnicity.

Justice: Working toward racial justice with investing requires increasing the amount of capital devoted to creating equita- ble outcomes for communities of color. Investments should use inclusive capital allocation to improve social, economic, and environmental outcomes for historically and currently mar- ginalized populations. These activities will create a more just society that allows for more equitable distribution of resources, and lead to more equitable outcomes between majority (often white) populations and populations that have been historically marginalized.

Included within each of these strategic goals are recom- mended indicators and metrics to guide investors on how to implement these recommendations into their investment strat- egies and set targets to hold themselves accountable to their racial equity commitments. You can learn more and see the indicators and metrics on GIIN's website, https://thegiin.org/.

CASE STUDY: PRIVATE EQUITY FIRM PROFITABLY PROMOTES EQUITABLE OUTCOMES

Private equity firms have a pretty straightforward business model: They buy a company and work with the management team to make changes in their operations to maximize efficiencies that they hope, leads to increased profits for the company, which can then lead to returns for the private equity firm or a sale to another company that brings in more money than the original firm spent. Like the holy trinity of capitalism, private equity can be a tool to help companies create a product or service that brings value to the lives of their customers and employs workers to create that value in exchange for a wage that offers a quality standard of living.

Not all private equity firms operate using the principles of the holy trinity of capitalism concept, but I know at least one that does, Jacmel Growth Partners. Jacmel is a growth private equity firm that focuses on acquiring and growing midsized companies grossing around $5 to $50 million each year. They specialize in family-run businesses, specifically those that offer business services to other companies. To date, Jacmel has deployed $45 million into five companies across two platforms.[34]

Jacmel's founder, Nick Jean-Baptiste, had a long career on Wall Street, where he oversaw over $10 billion in financing private equity transactions.[35] He decided to start his own firm, which he named after the small village in Haiti where his father was born, because he wanted to focus on investing in communities in addition to companies. Jacmel is "anchored to the values of reciprocity and care common in Jacmel village. The firm aims to treat all its partners, investors, and portfolio company employees as members of its community."[36]

Jacmel has redefined what it means to create a private equity partnership with a company, and takes a different approach with all the stakeholders involved.

TABLE 2.5 Jacmel Growth Partners vs. traditional private equity

	Traditional Approach	Jacmel Approach
Founders	• Founders transition out after acquisition • Executive team members replaced	• Value multigenerational relationships with families • Build on founder's vision • Expand management and board to include people of color
Investors	• Drive business decisions based on capital gains • Limited interest in community impact	• Have central focus on social impact • Support wealth creation for employees and their communities
Employees	• Not considered stakeholders • Not focused on impact of company outside of work	• Intentionally improve the well-being of families through various wealth creation and impact initiatives • Invest in employee skill building and advancing diversity and inclusion

Source: Jacmel Growth Partners

Critical to Jacmel's success is its "Office of Impact," which supports Jacmel to invest in employees to improve job quality, a company's bottom line, and its overall goodwill in the community when it acquires or invests in a company. The Office of Impact is managed in partnership with my firm, and deploys investment strategies in three areas:

1. **Wealth Creation:** Through the creation of an Option Pool companies put aside a certain percentage of stock in the company for nonexecutive staff to share. This gives employees greater incentive to perform as well as giving them wealth-building opportunities.

2. **Economic Mobility:** To do this companies strive to provide:
   a. **Workforce Development:** Hiring military service members and returning citizens who worked as civilian support staff
   b. **Education:** Providing college classes and professional training to employees
   c. **Career Opportunity:** Creating advancement opportunities for all employees
3. **Equity:** companies actively promote:
   a. **Diversity:** Recruiting and developing BIPOC (Black, Indigenous, and people of color) executives
   b. **Fair Pay:** Addressing institutional bias in pay
4. **Benefits:** Providing equitable benefit solutions for all employees. Offering these benefits to employees of acquired companies has not impacted their bottom line— it actually has improved it because it facilitated employee retention and growth as well as through reimbursements and incentives they receive from workforce development programs. (More on how investing in your people differently can help your bottom line in Chapter 4.)

Success Metrics

Despite taking this nontraditional approach to private equity, Jacmel has experienced the same performance level as similar private equity firms. Through its investments, it has created over $90 million in value, with their invested capital growing more than two and a half times within a few years. In addition to these financial metrics, they also track the number of families they have supported through their investments, which currently total over 800 and counting.[37]

Jacmel shows what is possible when we think innovatively— outside standard convention—within an industry. Often what we consider normal or a best practice is just an assumed way of doing things, and doing things differently can help unlock different business models and different ways to generate value. You may not be a private equity investor, but undoubtedly there are standard practices in your industry that can be re-examined to help you do well BY doing good.

What are those practices and how can you shift them to find new ways to make money and have an equitable impact in your industry?

3

Achieving Equitable Impact Through Your Spending

We give my son, Dylan, an allowance each week, and unlike your average 14-year-old, he doesn't go out and spend it immediately. Usually, he'll do one of two things with it: save it or invest it.

I don't know what we did raising him, but Dylan is very intentional about his money. He thinks a lot about where his money is going and what he wants to do with it. He's started to invest to grow his money and supplement his savings. He likes the idea of being able to buy something big later, rather than something small he wants right now. He's hoping that he can buy a Mustang one day with the returns from his investment portfolio. (Why a Mustang? Because of the *Fast & Furious* movies, of course. He's still a teenage boy!)

Delayed gratification isn't typical of teenagers, I know. But Dylan likes to be able to spend his money in the way he wants, and have the funds available to him to be able to do so. For example, we have a set amount we can spend on birthday presents for friends, but if there's something he knows his friend will like that's above our limit, he'll just cover the rest of the cost with his own money. He also is very focused on making sure he doesn't owe my husband and me any money, if he loses or breaks something. He plays a lot of sports and he's *constantly* losing his water bottles and buying new ones to replace them.

You may be wondering what the spending choices of a teenager has to do with your business. Well, in the same way Dylan makes decisions about how he spends his allowance, you are constantly making choices about how you spend your business's money. Every business spends money—as they say, you have to spend money to make money—but few think about the best ways to spend money beyond getting the lowest price for whatever they want to purchase.

To truly make an impact, the main course of your operations, you have to consider not only how you bring money into your company (discussed in Chapter 2), but what you do with that money as it goes back out. There is so much potential in a company's purchasing power, but few companies see their spending as a tool for impact and alignment with customer values. How your company directs its money says a lot about what your company truly cares about and the lengths it will go to make good on its promises to social causes. An excellent way to signal the authenticity and commitment to social impact that your customers crave is to literally put your money where your mouth is and fully integrate impact across your company's spending.

Dylan's intentionality with his allowance means that he can align his spending with his values. He values his friends, so he saves his money in order to give them what they want. He values his family, so he spends his money on things that will make our lives easier, like keeping me from losing my mind if he forgets his water bottle one more time at practice! And he values fast cars, so he's investing for the long term so he can get the car of his dreams when he can actually drive. (We'll see if we let him get that Mustang, even if he has the money.)

How is your company aligning your values with your spending? If you have a dollar in your (corporate) pocket, where's it going? Is it going right back out the door toward a cheap, flashy thing you think you need right now, or are you being intentional about what you do with it, so you are spending it on what you value?

This chapter will build on the previous one to help you understand how your company's spending can be an essential component of doing well BY doing good. In some ways, analyzing and shifting your spending habits is a relatively easy and straightforward approach to equitable impact. Most companies make hundreds if not thousands of spending decisions each month, and choosing a few spending decisions to test out opportunities for greater impact is a simple way to begin your journey toward greater values alignment. Since many spending decisions are visible choices—such as what kind of caterer or the types of products used at an event—it's an easy way to signal to customers that you understand their values and they are aligned with what your company cares about.

As in the previous chapter I will walk you through how to complete a second iteration of the Good Business Worksheet (Table 3.1), and you will see how the worksheet can help you understand how you are spending money and how you could spend those dollars in a smarter way that leads to greater impact. Then, we will examine a business case for spending with impact, illustrating how more intentional spending within communities can help increase economic growth and improve business for everyone. Then, I'll discuss the first step for analyzing your company's spending and suggest several areas of impact to consider involving your spending habits. The Innovate-Accelerate-Decelerate cycle will show you how to execute the different ways and the next steps to change your spending.

BUSINESS CASE: HOW YOU SPEND YOUR MONEY

The strongest business cases for integrating equitable impact into how you spend your money are the trends highlighted in Chapters 1 and 2: Your customers want you to be good. They want to trust that your company is aligned with their values and that you will execute them authentically. Your equitable impact goals cannot be authentic without considering how you spend your money and how that relates to what you are trying to do for society. There is a lot of upside potential in integrating equitable impact into your operations, as two-thirds of consumers want to buy from companies that create social impact.[1] But there is potential for downside too, if your company uses it as window dressing and doesn't integrate it throughout all your operations, including spending. Ninety percent of consumers say authenticity is a critical factor in their purchasing decisions.[2] Making a spending choice that runs counter to your stated values could lead to mistrust from your customers and a loss in engagement. If you are a company that has an explicit value around inclusiveness, but you have a vendor in your supply chain with a history of discrimination against LGBTQ individuals, your customers will see that partnership as a betrayal of your values.

These value alignment considerations are a huge reason for why you should be intentional about your spending decisions. But, in addition to these consumer-focused motivations, there is also a strong case for rethinking your spending to create broad, community-based economic benefits. Chapter 2 highlighted how people of color have less wealth because of generations of racist policies, which continues to limit their purchasing power. Well, the truth is that our country is becoming more diverse, and as our demographics change, economic opportunities are changing as well. Existing racial gaps in income and wealth[3] will have a significant impact on the overall health and vitality of our economy.

These racial gaps will lead to increasing income inequality, with greater amounts of money concentrated in the hands of fewer people. If there is less money to go around, or more money concentrated in the hands of the few, the result is less economic growth for everyone. Income inequality has been shown to slow economic growth: a 1 percent increase in the income of a country's wealthiest 20 percent is associated with a 0.08 percent lower GDP growth in the next five years. In the United States, the wage gap between Black and white people is responsible for as much as 0.2 percent of lost GDP each year.[4]

I am sure you are asking yourself, "What am I supposed to do about this?! You expect me to undo years of racism with only my company's budget? No way!"

Well, of course not. These are massive trends that will take massive coordinated public policy to undo, but there is a way for you to contribute to closing these racial gaps by using the tools offered through your company's spending habits. Your company is an engine of economic activity—for you, for its employees, and also for your community and the other businesses you choose to work with. Being more intentional about your business partners and suppliers can help them grow.

Business ownership and entrepreneurship are two of the best tools for growing the wealth of communities of color. According to the Association for Enterprise Opportunity, "The median net worth for Black business owners is 12 times higher than Black nonbusiness owners," regardless of their level of wealth before beginning a business. If Black businesses were fully resourced, the employment opportunities and resulting economic growth would be tremendous: if just 15 percent of Black-owned businesses are able to hire one more employee, the American economy could grow by $55 billion.[5]

But these communities face many barriers to fully participating in these wealth-building activities. Black-owned firms, for example, have lower-levels of revenue compared to firms in the same industry, and Black entrepreneurs are less likely to get a loan than their white peers, making it harder to branch out into new business areas.[6] Asian-American entrepreneurs also face barriers navigating the loan application process from traditional capital providers, forcing them to rely on personal capital, thus limiting their growth potential.[7]

As a business with money to spend, you can make an intentional choice to partner with businesses owned by people of color and help them grow and build wealth, which will further help build wealth for the communities in which they live. If you are having a staff meeting and need some catering, instead of working with the large corporate chain that you usually use for staff lunches, why not consider a smaller company that may need your business more? Instead of getting supplies from a large retailer, maybe there is a small local business that you can build a relationship with. Often, these types of companies are also eager for your business and will provide better customer service and work with you to better meet your needs.

Thinking about your spending as a contribution to the economic growth and development of fellow businesses will help you consider the broad impact of your spending—not only on other businesses, but also on your community.

FIRST STEP: THINK ABOUT THE IMPACT OF HOW YOU SPEND YOUR MONEY

Before you can begin to leverage your spending for equitable impact, you have to understand the *current* impact of your spending. Most companies don't consider how their spending affects their community or society—positively or negatively— and their vendor or procurement decisions are the result of personal relationships or habit—they have always worked with the same groups of companies. By analyzing where your money is going and where it could be going, you can start to increase your impact on those around you as well as increase your engagement with customers.

To be able to leverage the full impact of your spending, you have to shift your mindset and think of your business as a member of a community that is bigger than you and your employees. You are a part of a group of people, organizations, and institutions, and when one thrives, it helps everyone around you thrive. Even if you are a large company with offices around the country—or around the world—you still operate in specific places; you spend money in places where people live and work and play. That has an impact, whether you think about it or not. Like my son Dylan, you can be intentional about where your money goes, and change your spending patterns based on your values.

The ultimate goal here is to help your business become a good neighbor. You should see yourself as in partnership with the community or communities in which you work. Your business is an economic engine that can increase profits and earnings, but that does not happen in a vacuum. It affects and is affected by everything going on around it, from the hard work of your vendors and other partners and the compensation they receive to the community groups and government agencies that make where you work a nice, safe place. Once you see yourself as a partner in community health and well-being, it's easy to understand how changing your spending habits can help improve the places in which you operate.

VIRTUOUS CYCLE OF SPENDING AND GROWTH

The BOW Collective™ (short for Black Owner & Women's Collective) is an example of what could be possible when businesses think differently about company spending and how they partner with other businesses. Founded in early 2022, BOW is a collective of 50 businesses run by Black women, representing $200 million in annual revenue. The companies have come together to collaboratively compete for large-scale contracts from corporations and government agencies.

BOW was needed because Black women are frequently overlooked for major contracts or investment dollars that would help them expand their businesses. Only 0.3 percent of investment capital goes to businesses owned by Black women, and as a result, only around 1 percent of these businesses generate more than $250,000 in revenue.[8]

The members of BOW intend to leverage their connections and relationships with "Fortune 500 companies and government agencies to broker multi-year contracts," as well as create "stronger banking relationships and investment opportunities for their businesses."[9] The members have worked with clients like Amazon, GSA, the Department of Defense, Toyota, and Skanska.[10]

The formation of BOW comes as supplier diversity is increasingly a priority for large companies. A survey of large US and international corporations found that these companies expect to increase their diversity spending goals by 50 percent in the next three years, with 30 percent of them saying they set diversity spending goals for the first time.[11]

These companies want to partner more intentionally with firms they overlooked before, and the members of BOW are ready to partner with them. These partnerships with BOW and diverse suppliers generally will help these businesses grow and further invest in the success of their companies and their employees.

This virtuous cycle of spending and growth is possible everywhere, and any business can be a part of it. It doesn't require elaborate funding mechanisms or due diligence; any simple analysis of your spending can help point you in the right direction. Now, let's move on to the steps required to change your spending and help you be a better neighbor.

WHERE YOUR SPENDING CAN MAKE AN IMPACT

Once you've understood the need and value in being a good neighbor and aligning your spending to support it, below are a few areas you can consider when shifting your spending habits to be more impactful.

Vendors

The most obvious beneficiaries of your company's spending are your vendors and others you hire to help you run your company. A few things to consider:

- Who helps you implement your employee benefits?
- Where do you get your office supplies?
- Where do you purchase food for your employees or guests when you have lunch meetings?
- What about the year-end gifts that you get for your clients?

When you begin to think about all the different businesses *your* business works with, the list of possibilities for making an impact is almost endless. Maybe you can work with a local artist to design a new company logo or choose a more sustainable brand of paper for your printers. Changing your vendors is typically something you can shift easily and that can have an impact. Next time you have to choose a new vendor, think about who your dollars are going to and if they can go to someplace where they would make a greater impact.

Supply Chain

Another obvious area for impact intervention is your supply chain. Many companies, large and small, do not know the full social and environmental impact of their supply chain. Do you know how much greenhouse gas was emitted when making your product? Do you know the labor standards of your suppliers or the place where you bought your raw materials? Shifting the practices and partners within your supply chain is a bigger process than choosing a different place for the company dinner, so commitments in this area may take more time and energy. But changes in this area have the potential to make the highest impact, and have the added benefit of being the most visible commitments to social values in your customers' eyes.

Banking and Other Financial Services

If your business is bringing in money, chances are you are putting it in a bank somewhere. I know of very few entrepreneurs who are still using the "under the mattress" technique for their financial transactions. While banking services are technically not "spending," where you put your money and what you do with your funds can have an impact. You can have an account in a local community bank that actively invests in your community rather than international banks that may move your money anywhere in the world. If you have an investment portfolio or corporate treasury, you can use those funds to make impact investments, rather than focus only on return maximization.

You can take it a step further and actively use your corporate treasury accounts. Most businesses will keep some amount of funds in savings, mutual funds, or similar accounts, but you can also use excess funds to support your equitable impact goals. For example, McDonald's (not typically considered an investment firm), had a stake in Chipotle when it was still a Denver-based company, giving them cash to support their expansion.[12] Thinking about your corporate treasury in this way can help you and any company support a business who needs it and, if successful, generate profits for your business as well.

Employee Benefits

This is a little bit of a sneak peek into Chapter 4 (Achieving Equitable Impact by Investing in Your People), but employee benefits are another business expense that's worth considering as an area of impact. If you offer a 401(k) benefit to your employees, for example, you can offer investment opportunities in socially responsible funds. You could also be a little more innovative with your benefit structure, and offer incentives for volunteering; for example, additional vacation days, gift cards, or something else employees might value.

You can also think about the benefits you offer as an investment in your most valuable resource: your employees. You need to put your money where your mouth is when it comes to values, and the first place you should be doing that is with the people who make up your company. Treat your people like the asset they are with a competitive and strong benefits package.

Philanthropy

Many companies have some kind of philanthropic giving program. These programs are a great first step for creating an impact with your spending and being a good neighbor in your community. But you can take your philanthropic spending a step further by building off these philanthropic activities and integrating community support more deeply into your operations. Maybe there is a local nonprofit you can sponsor for a local fundraising ad campaign, or offer your services to them for free. Or maybe there's an opportunity to work with community groups to expand your talent pipeline and hire locally—something I'll talk more about in Chapter 4.

The Procurement Pipeline

Three of these areas of impact intersect to create what I call the "procurement pipeline": vendors, supply chain, and philanthropy. Although I present them separately to make it easier for you to understand how you can shift your spending habits, you should begin to think of them as the same or similar processes.

The pipeline works like this:

The companies that you work with in your supply chain are obviously your biggest partners and require the greatest amount of your time and investment. Because you are dependent on each other, you can influence them to create long-term equitable impact. Vendors are a step down from your supply chain partners, since they are likely to be smaller businesses that you can support and help grow with your spending. By working with vendors of color or other traditionally underinvested-in companies, you can help them reach the point where their businesses could become bigger partners in your (or other companies') operations and potentially one day supply chain partners

Community philanthropy is a part of the procurement pipeline because some businesses may not yet be at the level of partnering with you as a vendor or supply chain partner, and your philanthropic efforts can help build their capacity through training or other technical assistance. If you can't find the right partner with the appropriate capacity to meet your procurement needs, your community philanthropy can help grow and accelerate businesses to meet those needs. (Learn more about what this would look like in the "Spotlight On" section of this chapter.)

Considering your procurement activities in this way can help you be a good neighbor to other businesses by supporting them from their growth stage, to vendor stage, all the way up to a full partner in your supply chain. This is the kind of virtuous cycle that equitable impact is all about.

There is another version of the Good Business Worksheet titled "How you spend your money," which will walk you through these different areas of impact. As with "How you make your money," I usually work with full teams to implement these elements, and I recommend you do the same.

USE THE INNOVATE-ACCELERATE-DECELERATE CYCLE TO LEVERAGE YOUR SPENDING

Chapter 2 introduced the "Innovate-Accelerate-Decelerate" cycle as a way to implement the changes you would like to see in your company's business model to increase your equitable impact and trust with customers. You can apply the same cycle as you think about how to leverage your spending for equitable impact, although its execution is slightly different. Just like the earlier analysis in Chapter 2, you can use this cycle to innovate your current spending processes, accelerate what's already working, and reduce the more harmful aspects of your spending patterns.

Innovate

When considering your company's spending habits, innovation will focus on processes, which could come from within—through working with your employees or vendors based on opportunities they've identified—or you can bring new ideas into your own operations.

Let's use an example of innovative spending habits related to the "Employee Benefits" area of impact. In the past few decades, a growing movement of "impact investing" has begun to take hold within the financial services industry. The idea behind impact investing is that investors can achieve what are called double- or triple-bottom line returns: social, environmental, *and* financial. By making investments in solar power companies or companies that explicitly hire formerly incarcerated individuals, your money can create both a financial return and also improve society or the environment.

Impact investing is no longer a nascent trend within the financial industry. Most financial institutions have some kind of impact investing division, and consumers are more and more interested in putting their money into impact investing. These trends are more pronounced among younger millennial consumers; 95 percent of them say they are interested in more sustainable investing strategies.[13] Large pension funds have committed themselves to implementing impact investment strategies to better serve their members; for example, the California State Teachers' Retirement System committed to creating an investment portfolio that has a net of zero carbon emissions by 2050.[14]

If you've read this far, it probably won't surprise you to learn that there is absolutely no trade-off between regular investing and investing for impact. On average, impact investments do not perform any worse than more conventional investments. The Global Impact Investing Network found that impact investments had about a 5.8 percent average return, with the highest performing funds receiving over 20 percent returns and the lowest performing funds losing about 15 percent. This spread is about what you'd see in conventional investing, which means that doing well BY doing good is possible through investing.[15]

You can integrate impact investing into your employee benefits, allowing your employees options to choose impact investment funds for their 401(k)s or other retirement accounts.

If you have significant funds invested with a bank or other type of financial institution, you could consider shifting those funds into an impact-focused fund. One of your employees may be interested in helping to make this shift toward impact investing; it could be a professional development opportunity to lead a project and implement this kind of shift in your spending habits.

Accelerate

In Chapter 2, I discussed how expanding and accelerating what is already working in your company can help make equitable impact the main course of your operations. Here, acceleration can come fully from within, but you can also adopt proven practices from outside your company to help accelerate what you've already started. If the ideas presented previously around innovation are new pioneering and industry-leading concepts, opportunities for acceleration are things you can quickly expand on to respond to customer demands for greater equitable impact.

Like the innovation of impact investing, other companies and industries have been working on different ways to use spending for social change for years, even decades. Your company can learn from these practices, adapt them to your operations, and expand on them. Just because it wasn't your idea doesn't mean you can't build on it and make it your own. There were lots of superhero movies made before Marvel Studios started to make their own, but Marvel was able to smash box office records and redefine the genre with their own approach to it.

How can you take the Marvel approach to your company's spending? Accelerating something happening inside your company can help you expand your commitment to equitable impact. When I was the chief impact officer at Living Cities, a philanthropic membership organization of the world's largest foundations and financial institutions, we were beginning to grapple with our commitment and involvement in the racial justice movements growing across the country. We used public-private partnerships to support low-income people in cities, but had not necessarily acknowledged that most of those people were people of color. These communities face unique and specific barriers because of existing racist policies that could not be changed without confronting head-on the racism that people of color face each day.

We were late to the racial equity party, so to speak. So many organizations had been working on community organizing around racial justice for generations, and while we were working in these communities, we were not necessarily working in partnership around racial justice. Nevertheless, we were able to accelerate our journey by benefiting from the lessons learned from others.

One thing Living Cities did when deploying and applying their own organizational principles of racial justice was to analyze the impact of their spending, which led them to set targets around diversifying contractors and vendors. Living Cities created these targets after learning that businesses owned by people of color have a harder time accessing capital, and, therefore, have a harder time growing to a capacity where they can compete with larger companies in their industries.[16] By rejecting the status quo and intentionally seeking out and expanding their vendors and contractors of color, Living Cities provided needed revenue and business to firms that might not have access to contracts from similar organizations.

The barriers to capital access are particularly challenging for food service companies owned by people of color, which is one of the most volatile industries. When Living Cities realized that it was mostly using corporate chain stores to cater lunch meetings, they deliberately changed their default caterers to small businesses owned by people of color in order to better align themselves with their racial equity programmatic goals. It was a very easy thing to do and usually resulted in a tastier lunch![17]

Whom you choose to buy a company lunch from may seem like a small thing, but your vendor decisions can have a large impact, especially if you are a company with large amounts of dollars spent through your procurement processes. Whom you choose to work with also is a strong signal to your employees and customers. Having an immigrant-owned business do your company catering says something about the kind of company you are and can be a powerful marker for your company's culture.

The steps that Living Cities took to change its food vendors were important, but I don't want your takeaway to be that you just need to have different types of food at company lunches and you've done all you need to do to align your values with your customers. I've highlighted Living Cities because their changes in food vendors was a direct result of a broader strategy around racial equity, and their spending habits was one tool they used to meet those goals.

I wrote this book—and you are reading it—to help companies create a strategy that helps them do well BY doing good. If your company spends a lot on vendors but doesn't have a strategy for how to effectively partner with them as a good neighbor, consider a broader procurement strategy to actively work with and support your vendors. The Good Business Worksheet is meant to help you create that bigger strategy, not to offer a simple checklist for what your company needs to do. As I've said, authenticity is important. Customers can smell BS (or to paraphrase one of my favorite characters on *Ozark*—they can tell if you've got some BS in your teeth). If something aligns with your strategy, do it. If it doesn't, don't!

Decelerate

The deceleration process requires taking a hard look at what your company is doing and determining where you are doing more harm than good. What are you spending money on that you shouldn't be, or that you could be spending differently—that is, in ways that would be more aligned with your company's values and equitable impact goals?

It could be as simple as changing the paper in your printer to recycled paper, or spending less money on paper by changing the default printer setting to double-sided. Or, heck, don't use paper at all! Pretty much any purchase you make has some environmental impact, and there may be alternative products that are more environmentally friendly.

Tweaking the types of supplies you use in your office isn't a bad idea, but it would be hard to argue that these kinds of impact decisions are the main course; this seems more like a side dish or low-hanging fruit to me. If you are a company with an environmental mission or one that has made sustainability a core value, but are spending a large amount of money on paper and other disposable supplies, you probably should reconsider this practice and look for more sustainable options.

Where you can go big, and where there is opportunity for a lot of impact, is within your company's supply chain. If your company is making a product, the impact of that product can be large and far reaching, oftentimes spanning the globe. Let's say you are a midsized apparel company that sells kids shirts with unique designs. Most of your workforce is focused on design and marketing; you contract out the screen printing of those designs onto the shirts, and the shirt themselves are manufactured by a third-party company that works directly with the screen printer. It may seem like the only thing within your control is the choice of the screen printing vendor, but the reach of your spending is much larger than that. Does the shirt manufacturer follow fair employment practices, pay a living wage and benefits, and so on? And where does the fabric come from that goes into those clothes? Who makes it, and where do the raw materials come from?

At each step of the supply chain process, there are important questions to ask to ensure that where your money is going actually aligns with your corporate values. How are these vendors treating their employees? What are the working conditions at the different factories? What kind of impact do the materials used to make your product have on the environment? Are there harmful chemicals being used, affecting the workers and their community? How much greenhouse gas does the shipping process produce to get your clothes from the raw material stage all the way to the consumer?

As a midsized company, these questions may seem way outside the scope of what you can control. You have a direct relationship with one vendor, and they help you make the product you need, and you cannot really change what choices they make with their own purchasing decisions. But if you and your company have decided that environmental sustainability or fair labor practices are important, questioning your suppliers about these issues is an essential part of your equitable impact business practices. If the suppliers don't have a good answer, or they aren't willing to change their practices, you can always work to find a different supplier that is more aligned with your values.

If you are a large enough company with a big enough supply chain, you can shift from decelerating bad practices in your supply chain toward accelerating high-impact strategies across your spending practices. Supply chain management is an area ripe for intervention for social and environmental goals, and there are a lot of proven practices to learn from others.

LEVERAGE SPENDING FOR EQUITABLE IMPACT

Walmart is commonly cited to show how supply chains can be leveraged for impact. The ubiquitous retailer has committed to several environmental, social, and governance (commonly referred to as "ESG") goals, and is using its spending power through its supply chain to achieve those goals. Because

Walmart is one of the largest retailers in the world, its supply chain is one of the most massive economic engines on the planet. They are working to use that engine for social impact.

Walmart has set several goals to achieve with its supply chain, from climate change mitigation to respecting human rights to safer, healthier products. They have set standards for their suppliers around labor and environmental criteria, and are participating in advocacy groups that are pushing for socially impactful policies, such as the Renewable Energy Buyers Alliance, which is working to create a zero-carbon energy system. They are also moving toward working with smaller and more diverse suppliers based in the United States.[18]

You may not work at Walmart (or maybe you do!) and your company may not have the same level of purchasing power. Because of its size, you likely do not. But chances are you have more power than you think. You can join up with other companies with similar values to coordinate your efforts and learn from each other. The Renewable Energy Buyers Alliance helps coordinate activities for companies committed to environmental goals, and the group CEO Action for Diversity and Inclusion brings together companies committed to racial equity, with specific actions directed at supplier diversity.[19]

Regardless of your spending levels, the examples in this section may seem out of your reach or you may not be sure where to start. In the next section, I will walk you through the Good Business Worksheet to help you implement changes in how you spend your money for equitable impact.

PUT IT ALL TOGETHER AND CHANGE HOW YOUR COMPANY SPENDS MONEY

Table 3.1 is another iteration of the Good Business Worksheet, this time focused on how your company spends its money. As discussed, you can complete it by yourself, or with a team of

TABLE 3.1 Good Business Worksheet, Part 2: How you spend your money

How you spend your money

First Step: Understand the Impact of Your Spend	Innovate	Accelerate	Decelerate
In which areas of impact can you shift your spending habits? · Vendors · Supply chain · Banking and other financial services · Employee benefits · Philanthropy	*Which areas of impact within your company can benefit from innovation?*	*Which areas of impact can benefit from an acceleration of impact practices?*	*Which areas of impact in your company are doing more harm than good?*
What low-hanging fruit that would be easy to change can you identify?	*How will you bring innovative practices into these areas of impact?*	*How will you accelerate impact practices within these areas of impact?*	*What changes can you make in these areas of impact to decelerate the harm being done?*
What higher impact areas can you identify?	*What are your next steps toward implementing these changes across your company?*	*What are your next steps toward implementing these changes across your company?*	*What are your next steps toward implementing these changes across your company?*
	Will these changes affect certain groups more than others, and will they worsen or ignore disparities?	*Will these changes affect certain groups more than others, and will they worsen or ignore disparities?*	*Will these changes affect certain groups more than others, and will they worsen or ignore disparities?*

Download all the resources from this book at CapEQimpact.com.

coworkers; as I mentioned, I think it's best to do this with your team. I've also included a sample agenda (see Table 3.2) to help you walk through the different elements of the worksheet. (As always, you can find digital copies of these resources on CapEQimpact.com.)

TABLE 3.2 Good Business Agenda: How you spend your money

Time	Topic	Guiding Questions
5 minutes	**Business model alignment**	*What's the overall impact of your spending? Do you know where your money is going and why?* Note: This part of the meeting should be a quick review of your budget or other financial reports. If people need more time to understand your spending, give this section more time.
10 minutes	**Areas of impact**	*In which areas of impact are there opportunities to better align the company's spending habits with equitable impact?* Choose all that are relevant: • Vendors • Supply Chain • Banking and Other Financial Services • Employee Benefits • Philanthropy
15 minutes	**Low-hanging fruit and high impact**	*Where can we easily change things within these areas of impact that will give us quick wins on equitable impact?* *What are some opportunities that will require more time and resources, but will have higher impact long term?*
25 minutes	**Implementation plan: The Innovate-Accelerate-Decelerate Cycle**	Develop a plan of action by answering the following questions: • *How will you bring innovative practices into these areas of impact?* • *Which areas of impact can benefit from an acceleration of impact practices?* • *Which areas of impact within your company are doing more harm than good?* • *Will these changes affect certain groups more than others, and will they worsen or ignore disparities?*
5 minutes	**Next steps**	*What are your next steps toward implementing these changes across your company?*

Just like the Good Business Worksheet, Part 1: How You make your money, this worksheet is intended to help you easily map out how you can better leverage the money you spend for equitable impact. Once you are able to identify potential areas of impact, the Innovate-Accelerate-Decelerate cycle will help you implement whatever changes are possible within your company.

Some of these steps may overlap; that's OK, because it is more of an art than a science. However, you may want to think about the different components like this: innovate is about being a leader in your field or industry around equitable impact; accelerate is about expanding on good work already happening; and decelerate is about not doing harm. I'll push you, as I do my clients, to think about deceleration as not only "do no harm" with your company, but also as a way you can actually and actively do good.

When to Consider How to Spend Your Money

Just like with how you make your money, there are times that are better than others to consider your spending habits. I believe the best time to do this is when you are budgeting for the year or quarter, when you can do a full analysis of what you are spending and how you can shift some dollars to better align with your equitable impact goals. That doesn't mean you have to wait until then to do this—anytime you are making a purchasing decision, especially if it's a large one, is the time to think about how you can make a choice that will help embed equitable impact into your company. If you have an internal procurement team, or someone whose job is focused on contracts, set aside time to meet with them directly and go through the Good Business Worksheet so they can start implementing some of the recommendations.

Steps to Completing the Good Business Worksheet

Step 1: Analyze the full scope of your spending practices to better understand the impact of your spending. You could do a full budget analysis or simply list the areas of your biggest spending.

Step 2: Once you and your team have agreed on the broad outlines, you can go deeper into the different areas of impact within your spending:

- Vendors
- Supply chain
- Banking and other financial services
- Employee benefits
- Philanthropy

Some of these areas of impact may be more relevant to your company than others. If you are a service-focused company, there may not be a lot of opportunity within your supply chain, but you may have a large vendor base that can be considered for impact strategies. A smaller company may not have a robust employee benefits package, but could have a strong connection to the community with opportunities for greater community partnerships.

Once you have chosen your top areas for impact, circle them on the worksheet.

Step 3: With these top areas of impact circled on the worksheet, consider what may be some easy fixes that require a low lift from the team to increase impact. These should be things you can do in the next week or so—maybe switching to more sustainable products in the office, or choosing a vendor that's more aligned with your values. Write these opportunities down in answer to the low-hanging fruit question.

Now that you have your low-hanging fruit, think about things that may be more difficult, take a longer time, and require more resources to achieve, like overhauling your supply chain, or setting diversity goals for your procurement processes. Because these things take more from you and your company, they should produce really high impact results. Write these in answer to the high-impact question.

Step 4: Now that you have taken the first step toward understanding your spending and its areas of impact, you can move on to the Innovate-Accelerate-Decelerate cycle to help you implement your ideas about how to change your spending practices. Start with Innovate and consider which areas of impact would benefit from innovative practices, either created within your company, such as a new approach to choosing suppliers, or outside your company, like offering impact investing products as a part of your 401(k). These may be the answers you gave to the questions on the worksheet, or something else you and your team discussed.

Once you have identified the areas of impact that can benefit from innovation, write them down on the worksheet. Then, use the remaining questions in the Innovate column to help you figure out how to implement these innovative practices:

- *How will you bring innovative practices into these areas of impact?* Another way to think about this question is: What innovative strategies can help change spending habits in these areas?
- *What are the next steps to implementing these changes across your company?* To put it another way, what needs to get done to allow these changes to happen?
- *Will these changes affect certain groups more than others, and will they worsen or ignore disparities?* Don't forget about your blind spots—what are you missing in these decisions? What inequitable practice might this innovation inadvertently perpetuate?

Once you have the answers to these questions, write them on the worksheet. Remember, it's critical to actually physically write them down on this worksheet so everyone is aligned and you can use it as an organizing document for your next steps.

Step 5: Repeat this process for the next column as you consider what elements of your operations you can accelerate for greater impact. Which areas of impact would benefit from an expansion of something already happening within your company? Or is there a proven spending practice that you want to bring in to support changes within an area of impact? Again, write these areas of impact in the column, and then answer the following questions to help you make your implementation plan:

- *How will you accelerate impact practices within these areas of impact?* Or: What practices are in place that you can expand on to improve your spending practices?
- *What are your next steps to implementing these changes across your company?* Or: How can you support team members to implement these acceleration strategies?
- *Will these changes affect certain groups more than others, and will they worsen or ignore disparities?* Are all the people who will be affected by these decisions being consulted in the process?

Step 6: Almost done! Repeat this process for the "Decelerate" column. Choose the areas of impact you think can benefit from reducing some harm your company is doing, and answer these questions:

- *What changes can you make in these areas of impact to decelerate the harm being done?* Or what can you stop doing that would improve the impact of your spending?
- *What are the next steps to implementing these changes across your company?* Or what steps do you need to take to stop these practices from continuing?
- *Will these changes affect certain groups more than others, and will they worsen or ignore disparities?* Or who has

been most harmed by these practices, and how can they be empowered?

Don't forget to write everything on the worksheet!

Step 7: You did it! Share the completed worksheet with your team (or the whole company) and keep it handy. Begin to build out the different elements of the next steps as you shift your spending to better align with your company's values and create better impact.

In the next chapter, we'll round out the Good Business Worksheet and focus on how your company can better support its employees.

Spotlight On: Business Accelerators to Support Your Procurement Pipeline

Let's now explore the idea of the "procurement pipeline" to see how philanthropic spending can lead to business growth that meets the needs of your company.

Corporate and government contracts can be a huge boon to companies that can help them sustain and grow their operations. Receiving a large contract—like fulfilling a company's IT needs, or administering HR software for a government agency—can help a company significantly expand its business. But entrepreneurs of color frequently face barriers to bidding on and winning these kinds of contracts. One major barrier is the lack of access to capital to grow to a level where they can reasonably compete with similar businesses. These barriers include the rigid process of traditional underwriting, the high cost of capital for Black businesses and other businesses owned by people of color, and the lack of connections to financial networks.[20] They are also shut out of the more informal networks that lead to essential business relationships (think of the "old boys club" in a city that makes deals and business connections).[21]

One way to break down these barriers is to directly connect with these vendors and bring them into your procurement process or supply chain. However, because they have faced many barriers to success, businesses owned by people of color may not have the capacity to be able to meet the needs of your company.

This is where a business accelerator can support the growth and development of these companies to reach a size where they can effectively manage a multimillion-dollar contract. Business accelerators support small businesses with education, mentorship, connections, and increased access to financial resources. Those that explicitly target companies owned by people of color can help them overcome the barriers to their success and scale their operations and access larger contract opportunities.[22]

Supporting this kind of accelerator with your community philanthropy is a great way to build a pipeline of potential vendors if you are struggling to find companies that meet your equitable spending impact goals. Investing philanthropic dollars in an accelerator can lead to the development of a wide range of suppliers that you can partner with and help grow as your business grows.

The Brookings Institution, a think tank, has proposed what they call a "Minority Business Accelerator" grant program to support these kinds of accelerators around the country. The accelerators would target small businesses— at least $1 million in annual revenue—that can scale their operations to serve as suppliers to midsized to large companies, universities, and local and state governments, as well as hospital systems.[23]

This proposed model is based on the successful work of Cincinnati's Minority Business Accelerator, which has worked with over 65 companies to help them grow and access large spending contracts. The average company participating in the Cincinnati Accelerator has grown in size by $30 million, and about a quarter of them have doubled their size in three years, and, together, the portfolio of companies has created over 3,500 jobs and over $1.5 billion in average aggregate revenue.[24]

HOW YOU SPEND YOUR MONEY: SYDNEY'S JEWELRY SHOP

Let's check back in with Sydney and see how she's doing with the worksheet:

Step 1: She first thinks through her spending habits. She spends most of her money on the materials, but she also spends money on flyers to market her products; currently, she's also spending on a website in order to create an e-commerce sales channel.

Step 2: She doesn't have any employees (yet!) so that's not an area of impact, but the other areas I named seem to apply to her, although as a small operation without much spending, she's not sure how much impact she can have. But she wants to be sure she considers all her options.

Step 3: Low-hanging spending fruit for her includes buying recycled paper for her advertising flyers. This is easy and she's surprised she hadn't thought of it sooner. Something that's harder, but that she knows is going to have a big impact, is buying only from local businesses as she grows. Right now, she's not really able to choose the companies she works with—she has to go with the lowest price—but she wants to make sure she's helping to grow her community as she grows her business.

Step 4: Right now, Sydney is using a large, national bank. She decides to innovate by setting up an account with a community bank in the neighborhood that makes loans and investments in her community.

Step 5: For "accelerate," she decides she really wants to commit to revisiting her supply chain to meet the goal she set to create a carbon-neutral product. This was a big commitment, but now that she's looking at how she spends her money, she thinks there may be a simpler solution. She decides to shift from exclusively making plastic jewelry to relying more on wood and metals, and even materials she finds herself in nature, such as rocks and pebbles. (Her commitment to her supply chain shows how these different elements of the Good Business Worksheet can interact, meaning a commitment in one area can support a commitment in another.)

Step 6: For "decelerate," Sydney's decided to start working more directly with vendors in her community. She was using an international corporation for her website design; instead, she switches to a local web developer who lives nearby and can provide a more tailored approach to the e-commerce side of her business. It's a little more money, but better service and a more creative product.

Step 7: At each step of the Innovate-Accelerate-Decelerate cycle, she thinks through her blind spots and considers what she may be missing as she rethinks her spending. For example, under Innovate, she makes sure the local bank she will be working with lends to entrepreneurs who are unable to access traditional financing. For accelerate, she determines she hasn't any blind spots in her choice of materials—which is fine! Sometimes you won't have an answer to this question. What's important is that you think about it. For decelerate, she builds off her earlier commitments and finds a company that's a good fit with her values, not just one that advertises online—another example of how the worksheet components interact.

Step 8: Table 3.3 depicts Sydney's How you spend your money worksheet. Once she's done with this, she hangs it up next to the "How you make your money" version of the worksheet, and gets ready for the last section: how she invests in her people.

CASE STUDY: SPENDING FOR RECOVERY IN NEW ORLEANS PROMOTES EQUAL OPPORTUNITY

As we all know, Hurricane Katrina hit New Orleans hard. It's been years since that disaster, but while much of that city has recovered, many areas of the city and its people are still struggling.

Recognizing that New Orleans had a long road to recovery, civic and business leaders founded the New Orleans Business Alliance in 2010 to create economic opportunity across the city. The organization—referred to as NOLABA—focused on attracting and retaining businesses in the area, developing new small businesses, investing in neighborhoods, and implementing necessary workforce development training.

I started working with NOLABA in my role at Living Cities right around the 10-year anniversary of Hurricane Katrina in 2015. Despite lots of hard work and lots of dollars put into the recovery, there was still much more to do. Living Cities donated financing to NOLABA to support its work, and I helped them expand and manage their partnership with corporate leaders and government officials.

NOLABA was partnering closely with the city government and the mayor's office, particularly its Network for Economic

TABLE 3.3 Good Business Worksheet, Part 2: How Sydney's jewelry shop spends its money

How you spend your money

First Step: Understand the Impact of Your Spend	Innovate	Accelerate	Decelerate
In which areas of impact can you shift your spending habits? • Vendors • Supply Chain • Banking and Other Fnancial Services • Philanthropy *What low-hanging fruit that would be easy to change can you identify?* • Use recycled paper. *What are some areas for higher impact?* • Work exclusively with local vendors and businesses.	*Which areas of impact within your company can benefit from innovation?* • Banking and Other Financial Services *How will you bring innovative practices into these areas of impact?* • Use a local community bank. *What are your next steps toward implementing these changes across your company?* • Set up an account at the community bank and begin to shift all deposits to the new account. *Will these changes affect certain groups more than others, and will they worsen or ignore disparities?* • Use a bank that works with entrepreneurs not served by traditional financial institutions.	*Which areas of impact can benefit from an acceleration of impact practices?* • Supply Chain *How will you accelerate impact practices within these areas of impact?* • Use less plastic, relying more on wood, meta,l and found materials. *What are your next steps toward implementing these changes across your company?* • Collect materials from the woods and design new items based on these materials. *Will these changes affect certain groups more than others, and will they worsen or ignore disparities?* • NA	*Which areas of impact in your company are doing more harm than good?* • Vendors *What changes can you make in these areas of impact to decelerate the harm being done?* • Secure a new web designer that's local. *What are your next steps toward implementing these changes across your company?* • Set up an initial meeting with potential vendors. *Will these changes affect certain groups more than others, and will they worsen or ignore disparities?* • Seek a vendor with values alignment; don't rely just on internet research.

Opportunity initiative, which was working to create equitable growth strategies to ensure that economic development benefited all people, not just the wealthiest or most privileged. This equitable strategy was based on research that showed if all people of color throughout the New Orleans area had access to the same opportunities as white people, the state would see an additional $7 billion in earnings and $20 billion in economic impact.[25]

Most of the people and places that were hit hardest by Katrina and its aftermath were in the Black community. New Orleans lost about one in three of its Black residents in the aftermath of the storm,[26] and even 10 years after Katrina, about half of the city's Black residents said they had not recovered, compared to just a quarter of white residents.[27] NOLABA knew that to help create robust economic development across the city, they would have to fully invest in the Black community and its businesses.

Part of the challenge was that Black-owned small businesses had not had access to the opportunities that other businesses in the city receive. Even though about 40 percent of the small businesses in New Orleans are Black-owned, they received only 2 percent of the total receipts—a trend going back to the mid-1990s.[28] Without greater access to the city's economic activity, they are unable to grow and thrive at the same levels as other businesses.

To help solve this disparity, NOLABA worked with the city government to connect small, Black-owned businesses with developers and other companies supporting the Katrina recovery efforts. Billions of dollars were being spent to rebuild the city and NOLABA worked to ensure that those dollars stayed local, and that small businesses, particularly small businesses owned by Black people, were able to secure contracts to assist in that recovery.

The city also established a local hiring policy for these contractors to ensure that New Orleans residents could access and benefit from the jobs created. It also passed an employee and contractor minimum wage, raising it from $7.25 to $10.10 an hour, and adjusting it yearly for inflation. In 2021, it reached $15 an hour.[29]

By doing this, NOLABA created a multiplier effect from these development projects. The money spent not only went to the physical recovery of the city with new homes, buildings, and infrastructure, but also to local businesses and their local employees who supported their construction, either as direct contractors or subcontractors.

These and other efforts led to massive benefits for the city and its residents:

- Over 30,000 jobs created in the last 10 years.
- Three percentage point decrease in unemployment rates over the last 10 years.
- In 2019 alone, $8.5 million in contracts awarded to entrepreneurs of color.[30]

These results are not only because of the work NOLABA did to direct spending and contracts to small businesses, but also because of their broader equitable strategy to ensure all can benefit from the economic activity in New Orleans. This strategy incorporated all elements of the Good Business Worksheet—making money through sustainable development; spending money in a way that helps small businesses thrive; and investing in people through higher wages. The procurement and contracting efforts were (and are) a major pillar of their approach, and show what's possible when you think more intentionally about how you spend your money, where you spend it, and who you spend it on.

Even if you aren't working with city governments and major developers, how can you use your spending differently to create the kind of equitable impact NOLABA was able to create?

Achieving Equitable Impact by Investing in Your People

L et's go back to the digital imaging company, Doc-Scan, I introduced in Chapter 2. You may remember, I had walked them through a series of recommendations using the Good Business Worksheet framework, and suggested that they implement more environmentally focused business strategies as a way to distinguish themselves among their competitors and access new market share.

They did not go for it. They saw an environmental focus as outside their Equitable Impact Venn Diagram. Sometimes a recommendation that makes sense on paper just does not fit well with a company's sense of shared identity. Doc-Scan did not see itself as an environmental company and did not want to go in that direction. It wasn't that they hated the environment and spent the company retreat burning huge bonfires of paper—it just ran against who they thought they were, and they did not feel like they had the tools or resources to make that shift within their core business operations. This testing of the recommendations is an important part of the process, because if the equitable impact strategies do not seem authentic to the company, they will definitely not seem authentic to customers.

Because we walked through all three components of the Good Business Worksheet—how you make your money, how you spend your money, and how you invest in your people—shifting to an environmental business model wasn't the only recommendation I made to help their company do well BY doing good.

I also reviewed their HR policies and employee benefits packages and identified a few opportunity areas where they could treat their employees a little bit better and also save some money in the long run. Doc-Scan relied on a mostly low-skill workforce to do the manual labor involved in the document scanning process. They offered good jobs to their employees, but the nature of the job created high turnover rates and sometimes unreliable employees. Turnover is a standard challenge in Doc-Scan's industry and similar industries, and creates a lot of excess expense for the company. A more reliable workforce would save them money.

We identified this challenge in our conversations, and I suggested an opportunity to consider was how they could invest more resources in their workforce in a way that could produce long-term benefits. Intrigued, Doc-Scan's leadership and I began to work on strategies that would help increase retention while also helping improve the lives of their employees—things like on-the-job education, pathways to promotion, and management training. As I'm writing this, Doc-Scan has reported some preliminary positive results from these changes, with employees who participated in the training receiving promotions, which led to increased retention.

The Doc-Scan strategy illustrates the potential of the third and final component of the Good Business Worksheet: Part 3. Improving how you treat your people can help improve your bottom line. For some companies, it is obvious that employees are the core resource of any company, and investing in them is no different than investing in any other revenue-generating resource. But some companies don't necessarily see it that way, or haven't fully understood what it takes to invest in people in a way that produces benefits for their workforce and bottom line.

Some companies also distinguish (explicitly or not) between low-wage, entry-level employees and higher-paid salaried roles. They see the low-wage workers as interchangeable expenses, whereas they see the higher-paid salaried workers as assets and invest heavily in their success and growth. This chapter will show you that investing in all your people as the assets they are can lead to equitable value creation.

By "investing in your people" I don't mean just your employees. You also have to think about potential employees and talent that you haven't accessed yet. As I discussed in Chapter 3, doing well BY doing good requires your company to be a good neighbor. As a good neighbor, you should think about how the economic engine of your company is supporting the growth of your community. One easy way to do that is to hire people from that community.

In this chapter, I will walk you through the third component of the Good Business Worksheet. Some of the recommendations may seem obvious if your company has a robust company culture that aligns with strong company values. I won't go too deep into the business case for why a good corporate culture that values people leads to a company's success, as there are so many great thinkers and writers focusing on this topic. (Not sure I can top Peter Drucker's famous maxim, "Culture eats strategy for breakfast.") Instead, I will focus on how treating your employees differently (and better) can support the growth of your business while also having an equitable impact in their lives and the lives of their communities.

Even though this is the last section of the worksheet, do not think of it as the last step. As we saw, how Doc-Scan invested in its people was actually their entry point into the concept of doing well BY doing good. For many readers, this chapter may resonate more than the others. To fully reap the benefits of doing well BY doing good, your company must analyze all its practices with an eye toward equitable impact. Truly making equitable impact your main course throughout all your operations will inspire a greater trust from your customers, increase brand loyalty, and help you expand your business. You cannot have this thorough approach to equitable impact by picking and choosing only what you want to focus on and ignoring what you don't care about.

BUSINESS CASE: HOW YOU INVEST IN YOUR PEOPLE

There is a pretty straightforward and obvious business case for investing in your people—it saves you money in the long run. You do not want your employees to leave your company and have to replace them because that will cost you money—potentially a lot of money. Depending on the type of worker, the cost for hiring and replacing an employee could range from thousands to hundreds of thousands of dollars. For hourly workers, hiring a new employee could cost around $1,500. For a technical job, it could be one to one and a half times the annual salary. For C-suite executives, the total cost could be over *twice* the annual salary, or more.[1] This is not just the direct cost of hiring an employee (i.e., the cost of advertising or a recruiter's fee), but also things like the cost of lost productivity and training a new hire.[2]

These hiring costs are high, and if you are running a small-to medium-sized business, they could be a huge drag on your operation. But you can do something to reduce these costs: in a survey of 34,000 employees, the Work Institute found that 75 percent of the causes of employee turnover were preventable.[3]

The turnover problem—which by some estimates costs the entire US economy $1 trillion a year[4]—is really a problem of employee engagement. The best thing you can do to reduce your turnover and retention costs is to make sure your employees are happy and engaged. Gallup did research that showed only 15 percent of employees around the world feel engaged in their work, and around half are looking for new jobs.[5] This trend is more acute for the millennial generation. In a different study, Gallup found that 60 percent of millennials are open to a new job and their generation is the most likely to switch jobs.[6] The Great Resignation and the tightening labor market has only accelerated trends that were already underway.

Employers can increase engagement and employee satisfaction in many ways, but the big ones are compensation and benefits. Thirty percent of employees say that they switch jobs because of pay, and around 40 percent say that good benefits and paid time off are a motivator for staying at a job for more than five years.[7] Work culture is also super important: a 2018 LinkedIn study found around half of employees want to work for a company with flexibility and work-life balance, as well as one that has a welcoming culture.[8] The premium placed on flexibility has only increased during the pandemic, with a 2021 study finding that around two-thirds of employees prefer to work from home rather than the office, and 85 percent prefer jobs with remote work options and the flexibility that offers.[9]

Companies tend to not think of their social impact initiatives as an opportunity for employee engagement, but it has the potential to become one of the biggest leverage points for increasing retention and employee happiness.[10] The LinkedIn study found around half of employees want to work for a company that has a positive impact on society.[11] Over half of employees say that having a job where they can make an impact is important to their happiness, and those who feel that they are making a social impact through their job are twice as likely to be satisfied with their employer than those who are not.[12] These numbers hold up, too, when you look at the specifics of what makes people feel that their work is having an impact:

if they've worked on a specific social impact product, contributed to a social responsibility campaign, or volunteered at work through a community partnership.[13]

Not surprisingly, these trends are starker for millennials, and, as they age into being the majority of the workforce, social impact will become an even more critical tool for employee engagement. Deloitte found that millennials who frequently participate in workplace volunteer activities were twice as likely to be satisfied with the progression of their careers.[14] Net Impact—a membership group of social impact professionals— found that over half of students were willing to take a pay cut to work for a company that had similar values to theirs, and 45 percent were willing to take a pay cut for a job that made a social and environmental impact.[15] This was a survey of students about to enter the workforce, which means that as younger professionals join the workforce, the pressure felt by companies from their employees to align more with social impact will continue to grow.

This should be evidence enough to make you consider how you are treating your people in order to increase retention (I'm sure your company has already made trade-offs between offering a strong compensation and benefits package to attract and keep good employees with the cost of doing so). One area many businesses don't pay much attention to is the other component of who makes up "your people," by which I mean not just your employees, but the broad pool of potential employees.

If you expand your notion of who could be a potential employee, you'll be surprised at the benefits to your company. For example, anyone with a criminal record is usually automatically removed from a hiring search, but actively recruiting from this population and supporting them in their employment can be a win-win for them and your company. People who have been involved with the justice system, who have been homeless, or who have been struggling with addiction all face challenges getting a job and staying employed. People returning from prison are five times more likely to be unemployed,[16] which leads to a greater chance of returning to prison. By some estimates, the cost of just one former prisoner going back to prison can be as much as $150,000.[17] Employing them can help save society money, give someone who needs it a good job, and create dedicated employees for your company.

Greyston Bakery, for example, which produces brownies for consumers as well as for companies like Whole Foods and Ben & Jerry's, has what they call an "open hiring" policy. They do not ask for résumés or do background checks. While this may seem radical, it's worked for them: they have a 12 percent turnover rate, compared to 30–70 percent in similar industries.[18]

Dave's Killer Bread, the bread manufacturer, also works explicitly to hire justice-involved individuals. Around a third of their team members have a felony conviction. The company has had so much success with their program that they started what they call the Second Chance Employment playbook for other companies to use. So far, over 1,000 other companies have benefited from their lessons in working with this population.[19]

Your average person would not consider justice-involved individuals or those who are unhoused to be model employees, but that's just an assumption and prejudice we hold, not a fact. Reconsidering who your people are and how you treat them can help increase the engagement of your workforce and save you money on turnover and retention.

In my experience, the best way to improve how you invest in your people is to look at your company values and see how they align with your corporate practices and operations.

FIRST STEP: CONSIDER YOUR VALUES ALIGNMENT

Companies most often work to create a strong corporate culture by defining it through a series of "core" or "company" values. Your company probably has a list of these; they're probably similar to those at other places you've worked: Excellence. Respect. Boldness. Trust. Fun. Sound familiar? These trends in corporate values makes sense because most people want similar things. We want to work in a place where we feel respected. We want our customers taken care of, we want to do good work, and we want our company to prosper.

But values can be static and generic. In the effort to boil them down to universal truths, values are often universally useless. Many leaders and businesses try to create a list of values to impose upon the company, instead of creating a company with those values woven into the fibers of the business. They take the same approach to people: hire folks who have the skills they need and then try to instill the values in them once they are on board rather than hiring people who, themselves, embody the values.

It is so important that values remain a dynamic element in your company. Without continually looking at your values, you risk them becoming meaningless. I've talked a lot in this book about aligning your values with your customers, but you also need to consider how your values align with your employees. How are you living those values in your internal culture?

In Chapter 3, I asked you to make a mindset shift around your spending habits and think about how you can be a good neighbor in your community. In this chapter, I'm going to ask for another mindset shift: to consider whether you treat your people like a commodity or like an asset. You frequently hear discussion of "human capital" in the same way people discuss "physical capital," but your employees are living, breathing individuals that are not interchangeable like factory equipment. In many ways factory equipment is treated better than employees in the way they are treated on a company's financial statements. Equipment is classified as an asset on the balance sheet, which incentivizes long-term investment. Meanwhile, employees are treated as expenses on the income statement, which encourages divestment away from human capital.

You're probably reading this and thinking, *of course,* I treat my employees like the special, unique individuals they are. And you probably do, or at least think you do. But, if you want to truly do well BY doing good, you have to think about how you are living your values every day, and what you can improve. How do you create a company culture and a dynamic set of values that invests in your people as the assets they are?

Our values were actually one of the first things I had in place before I started my company. I wanted a vision for the kind of company we were, and how we wanted to treat our employees, and then built a business around that. These values were based on the belief that everyone, no matter who you are or what your circumstances, wants to Live.Learn.Grow.™ Our goal as business owners is to cultivate an environment for employees to live fully, learn constantly, and grow into their potential. This is the kind of dynamic culture that creates a successful business.

From the Live.Learn.Grow. culture I was able to develop what I call the Values Snowball™ (see Figure 4.1), which illustrates an explicit connection between values and purpose that reinforces the Why of our organization, which inevitably influences How we do the What.

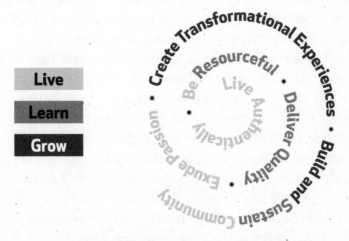

FIGURE 4.1 The Values Snowball demonstrates the impact a business can have on the world.

As I developed the Values Snowball to ground my company's values, a few things were critical to me; my values must be:

- Action-oriented
- Relevant—regardless of tenure or stage in the organization
- Dynamic—they grow, change, and develop with individuals
- Holistic—they apply personally and professionally

This led to the company values depicted in the snowball:

- Live authentically
- Be resourceful
- Deliver quality
- Exude passion
- Create transformational experiences
- Build and sustain community

Companies are beginning to understand the mindset shift of investing in a strong growth culture for employees; this was especially true after the COVID-19 pandemic upended the labor supply. Companies like Starbucks, Target, Walmart, and Amazon began or increased tuition reimbursements for employees. Investing in employees' growth and learning helps secure their workforce and creates a better, values-aligned culture that supports the long-term health of their company.

As we saw in Chapter 3, making decisions that conflict with your stated company values can hurt your credibility with customers and decrease their trust in you. If you have a stated company value of "respect" but your managers are disrespectful to their subordinates, that is going to cause you problems. Customers won't want to support that, and employees are going to leave, leading to higher turnover and increased costs.

In the rest of this chapter, I will walk you through how to ensure that you are actually *living* your company values, not just talking about them at the occasional corporate retreat. Even a company with a strong corporate culture and happy employees can identify changes they should make in their internal practices to help them do well BY doing good more effectively. That's an important element of the Live.Learn.Grow. culture—there's always an opportunity to do more to support your people and increase your impact.

WHERE TO MAKE AN IMPACT BY INVESTING IN YOUR PEOPLE

There are a few areas of impact to consider when thinking about how to better live your values and align your corporate culture with what kind of company you want to be:

Recruitment

The introduction to your company culture begins with your hiring process. Where do you look for new employees and strong talent? What does your recruitment process look like from start to finish? What is the experience for potential employees, whether they are hired or not? Oftentimes, people look to hire people who look and act like them.[20] In addition to excluding a broad group of people from becoming part of your company, it has implications for your productivity—diverse teams are usually better performing teams.[21] Confronting biases in your hiring process can help you make changes and become more inclusive and benefit from all the talent that's out there.

Training and Promotion

Once your people are in the door and working for you, are you investing in their growth and education? We all know the phrase "dead-end job," and there's nothing worse for morale than an employee who feels stuck with nowhere to go. Offering a growth path to taking on more responsibilities and more senior roles can do wonders for your company culture. If you aren't large enough to have enough jobs for a robust promotion strategy, you can still give employees professional development and help them create a career path, whether inside your company or not. Making these investments is particularly important if you have started to broaden your talent pool like Greyston or Dave's Killer Bread, and are working with people who may not have had a lot of formal employment experience. Giving these employees the training and support they need is a critical component of supporting their success and the success of your business.

On-the-job training or formal apprenticeships are a great way to build the talent of your team and think differently about who can and should be working with you. Often this kind of training has no out-of-pocket expense and can be a good opportunity to encourage your staff to take on formal leadership and management roles.

Compensation

Compensation is an obvious area of impact for how you invest in your employees—the more you pay them, the happier they are! Who doesn't like to make more money? While generally true, in actuality, the amount of compensation sometimes is not as important as the relative compensation between people. (This assumes, of course, that you are paying your employees enough for them to make a decent living, as well as an amount that's competitive for your industry.) If you are paying two different people different amounts of money for the same job, you need to make some changes quickly. I am sure you have read many exposés about companies who were paying men more than women for the same job, or people of color less than white people. You don't want anyone to write these stories about you.

Diversity, Equity, and Inclusion

When you look at your staff, what do you see? Do you see similar faces, or do you see a lot of different types of people all committed to making your business the best it can be? As I said when discussing the impact of recruitment, people tend to hire people who look like them. Making a commitment to diversity can not only open you up to new talent pools, but to people with different types of experiences that reinforce and strengthen your team. As demographics shift and the consumer market becomes more diverse, you want a diverse staff that reflects your customers. Creating a plan to diversify your talent pool can include things like using a recruiting firm that specializes in diverse recruitment, or working directly with alternative job training programs like Year Up.

The flip side of recruiting a diverse staff is creating a more inclusive company culture. Oftentimes when a traditionally white organization or team begins to implement diversity strategies, new members can feel excluded or not listened to. Intentionally building out an inclusive culture can help diverse teams thrive. There are many established strategies for increasing diversity, equity, and inclusion (DEI), and there are many trained consultants you can bring in to help you create and maintain a welcoming culture.

Creating this welcoming culture is becoming increasingly important. Companies have made a lot of progress in addressing racism at work, but there are still issues. According to an Edelman survey, more than half of employees—45 percent of white people, 64 percent of black people, 68 percent of Latino people, and 58 percent of Asian people—say that racism has harmed their employer relationship. In 2021, the lack of an inclusive culture was the biggest concern among employees, beating out lack of diversity as a top concern.[22]

Increasing diversity and demand for inclusivity leads to challenges that companies struggle to overcome: 64 percent of organizations say building diverse and inclusive teams is a primary concern, but only a third are intentionally creating inclusive and diverse teams, and a little under half are supporting their leaders to create inclusive cultures.[23] The increased demand for remote work can lead to benefits and challenges around creating an inclusive work culture: it can create flexibility and help your company recruit beyond your typical employee profile, but can also lead to a "proximity bias" in which those who put in more face time in the office are rewarded, either subtlely or explicitly. Intentionally building in structures to help counteract this bias can ensure all employees are fully integrated into the company culture and operations.[24]

Benefits

Like compensation, benefits are an important component of investing in your people and creating an engaging and sustaining corporate culture. A strong benefits package will attract top talent and help keep them working for you.

Of course, a strong benefits package can be expensive. There are always trade-offs when considering the size and type of compensation package you provide. Depending on your company values and culture, you can offer different or innovative types of benefits that may not cost much out of pocket: days off for volunteering, for example, or discounts on health classes, financial literacy courses, or other educational resources. The flexibility to work from home is an increasingly valuable benefit in a post-pandemic world and won't cost your company much, if anything.

Interestingly, but maybe not surprisingly, this area of impact intersects with choices you make in the "compensation" area. You can save money on your compensation and benefits package, if you offer more flexibility as a benefit. Around 60 percent of workers would be willing to take a pay cut for a remote work option, and 70 percent would give up other benefits like health insurance or paid time off for flexibility around coming into the office.[25]

And there are other benefits you can offer employees that can improve their quality of life and create equitable impact:

- You could partner with a service provider to improve the financial health of your employees. Companies like SmartPath work with companies to offer their employees a "financial coach" to help them better understand their spending and saving habits, and create more financial security for themselves and their families.
- You could set up an Income Advance program, which offers employees small ($1,000–$2,000) same-day loans that are paid back at their next paycheck. This can be a huge help to employees who experience a financial emergency and create more financial flexibility. (This is a great improvement over what are known as "payday" loans, where money is lent at a high rate of interest, with the idea that the loan would be paid back on the next payday.)

  Rhino Foods, a manufacturer of specialty desserts, in partnership with B Lab, created the "Income Advance Guide" to help other companies implement the program. They saw the benefits to their employees and wanted to encourage others to adopt the practices.[26]

Innovative services like SmartPath and Income Advance have obvious benefits for entry-level and frontline employees, who may be lower-income and struggling to make ends meet. But, they also benefit all types of employees regardless of their income level. You never know who will benefit from these kinds of products. As you think about your values, consider what innovative options may be out there to help you meet those values. If you think of your company like a family, and families look out for each other, you may want to create some kind of loan services for employees in need. If you value fiscal responsibility, a service that helps increase your employees' financial literacy may be a good fit for your company.

Employee Ownership

Employees are critical to your company's success, and if you want to give them more responsibility for the success or failure of the company, consider employee ownership options. These range from basic profit-sharing incentives (many companies offer stock options) to forming a co-op with equal ownership among all employees. Co-ownership with employees can be a huge shift in your operational model, and comes with tax and legal implications, so steps toward employee ownership should be thoughtfully considered and involve many stakeholders.

Table 4.1. Good Business Worksheet, Part 3: How you invest in your people is the third iteration of the worksheet. The corresponding agenda (Table 4.2) will walk you through it with your team. The rest of this chapter will take you through the Innovate-Accelerate-Decelerate cycle one last time to help you figure out which areas of impact you can work on to improve how you work with and support your employees.

THE INNOVATE-ACCELERATE-DECELERATE CYCLE FOR INVESTING IN YOUR EMPLOYEES

As with the previous two chapters, we'll once again go through the Innovate-Accelerate-Decelerate cycle to help you implement all the recommendations in this chapter in a way that makes sense for your company.

I call it a cycle for a reason: you and your company should always be thinking about it and considering what you could and should be innovating on, accelerating, and decelerating. The hardest cycle will be the first; it gets easier after that. Just like you probably have a continuous improvement process or periodic quality control checks, you should have a continuous improvement culture around your impact strategies. The Good Business Worksheet and the Innovate-Accelerate-Decelerate cycle can help you not only as you start this process, but also as you continue thinking about increasing your equitable impact as your company grows and expands.

Innovate

Here, I'll use a personal story to show what being innovative can do to support your employees. I gave birth to my daughter while I was working at a job that required a lot of travel. I was on the road almost every week when I returned to work, leaving my baby at home. I was still breastfeeding, so I had to take my pump with me.

Once I was in an airport, trying to get home, and I needed to pump. There was nowhere I could do it in private. I looked and looked around the terminal, but nothing. (Thankfully, this is less of an issue now as many airports have lactation rooms for new mothers.) I ended up in the bathroom, in a stall, with the pump balanced on my knees.

Needless to say, I was not pleased. In addition to having to catch a flight, I also had dozens of emails to respond to, calls to make, work to do. I did not have time to rush around a terminal looking for a private place, find nothing, and then sit in a bathroom stall trying not to spill milk on the floor.

I was an executive struggling with this problem, and couldn't imagine what a new mother with a low-wage job (or two or three) had to go through to provide breastmilk for her baby. Retail and service workers often have unpredictable schedules, low wages, and little opportunity for advancement. These jobs are hard and undervalued, and do not offer the opportunity for employees to assert their needs around things like breastfeeding.

Thirty states now have laws supporting breastfeeding in the workplace,[27] but there are still so many barriers for retail workers, entry-level workers, and any type of "frontline" worker who regularly interacts with customers to do this. If I had to name one type of employee who is seen as an interchangeable commodity rather than an asset to be invested in, it's these workers.

We need to think differently about how we invest in our employees and the structures we set up for them, especially for low-wage and entry-level workers. I faced so many challenges as a new mother, and those challenges are magnified for people with less privilege and support than I had. If you employ these kinds of workers—either in a retail store, a call center, or something similar—there are some innovative practices you can implement to help support them, improve their lives, and increase your bottom line.

The social impact consulting firm FSG, as part of their Talent Rewire initiative, researched the economic consequences of how our current system treats entry-level retail employees. (Disclosure: I consulted on some components of the Talent Rewire work.) They found that the retail industry loses $9 billion every year to turnover of entry-level employees. They looked into practices of companies like Verizon Wireless, the Container Store, and others to identify four strategies to increase retention and advancement of retail workers (see Figure 4.2).[28]

Investing in these kinds of innovative strategies to support your frontline or entry-level workers can improve their lives while also helping your company. The FSG research found that if a person doesn't have a steady job by the age of 25, they're at risk of losing around 40 percent of their lifetime income.[30] Investing in young workers early and helping them keep up their employment can have a huge impact on their overall quality of life. It can also have a huge impact on your business, as high-performing companies are 1.5 times more likely to offer entry-level employees the chance to advance in their careers than lower-performing companies.[31]

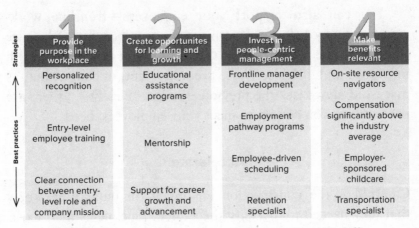

FIGURE 4.2 Strategies for investing in entry-level talent[29]

About 9 million of the 24 million frontline employees (defined by FSG as "entry-level employees who engage closely with customers") are people of color. These people "represent a reservoir of talent, innovative ideas, and multicultural competency that are increasingly sources of competitive advantage."[32] Just as we have to think differently about how we support frontline employees generally, we also have to pay special attention to how we support our frontline employees of color. Many of these workers face additional barriers to success due to the effects of racism on their lives and their families. All of the steps outlined in Figure 4.2 can help support these types of employees, but you also must work to create a racially inclusive company culture.

FSG and PolicyLink did further research on supporting frontline employees of color and found three areas companies can invest in to create a more inclusive company culture for people of color: "building internal capacity for an inclusive, understanding, and adaptive culture; strengthening management and HR systems, policies, and practices; and intentionally investing in the development, recognition, and promotion of frontline employees of color."[33]

You can also support your employees—frontline workers or not—by being innovative with your benefits. When we think about benefits, we typically think about things like health insurance and 401(k)s. Those are important, of course, but, as discussed above (see the previous section "Benefits"), there are other things you can do to meet your employees' needs.

Accelerate

Caterpillar, the construction equipment manufacturer, knew that they needed to diversify their talent pipeline as their existing workforce reached retirement age and the labor market grew increasingly competitive. But a manufacturing skills gap among young people and recent graduates meant they were struggling to find qualified applicants to meet their workforce needs.

I worked with Caterpillar to help them pilot a solution to this problem in Peoria, Illinois. This community in particular needed quality jobs; at the time, almost 20 percent of its Black residents were unemployed, compared to the national average of 4 percent. The community needed jobs, and Caterpillar needed employees. Seemed like an opportunity ripe for equitable impact!

Caterpillar worked with the public school system to develop a new curriculum to support essential and technical skill development. They worked directly with a high school that had a manufacturing focus to recruit students who were interested in gaining paid experience in manufacturing, while also receiving professional and personal mentorship along with academic credit.

Seven students completed the initial pilot program, and four were hired full time. Caterpillar expanded the program to four additional school districts in the fall of 2018 and expanded the focus from manufacturing to all STEM areas. The Peoria school district found the curriculum training so successful they expanded parts of it to the entire district.[34]

Caterpillar's results show that your company can easily accelerate these activities and expand your talent pool by recruiting and investing in young people who do not have a formal college education. Many of them are from lower-income backgrounds and are also more likely to be people of color, and, therefore, may have faced many barriers to success. An internship or apprenticeship with your company could be life-changing for them and their families. Success with this population requires rethinking your employee support structure as well. For this reason, the recommendations concerning support staff of color in the innovate section of the worksheet are relevant if you are looking to accelerate by emulating Caterpillar's success.

There are likely many community groups that work with recent graduates or other young people looking for work, and you can offer your own on-the-job training to mirror the job skills education that the Caterpillar program provided. These kinds of apprenticeships, not internships, are a great investment as well. Only about a third of employers have apprenticeship programs, but those that do are much more likely to be successful companies: high-performance organizations are 4.5 times more likely to have an apprenticeship program or say they are going to start one, according to the Institute for Corporate Productivity.[35]

Decelerate

I won't spend too much time on this section, because I hope the recommendations here would be obvious to you by now; you should decelerate any practices that harm or hurt your employees. If you aren't paying your employees a living wage, start paying them what it takes for them to take care of themselves and their families. If you are paying two people different salaries for the same job, fix that as soon as you can.

This may seem like an easy step, but if you are guilty of any of these practices, it will take time and energy to make amends. The National Low Income Housing Coalition found that currently there is nowhere in America that a full-time minimum wage worker can afford to pay rent. That's right—if you work full time at the minimum wage, you do not earn enough to pay for a roof over your head. The average worker needs to make $20.40 an hour to afford a one-bedroom apartment, and $24.90 for a two-bedroom.[36] Depending on your company, paying this much may be easy, or it may be a stretch. As of this writing, the highest minimum wage in the country was $14.00 in California,[37] where housing is even more expensive— the average monthly rent in California was around $1,900 in 2021, more than 50 percent higher than the national average. Housing costs vary across the country and can be much higher within states themselves. For example, the average rent for an apartment in San Francisco, California, is more than twice the state average at $4,200 a month.[38]

You may not think there are any wage disparities in your company and that everyone is receiving a fair wage or salary for their work. This is actually hard to determine—the wage gap between men and women, or white people and people of color, isn't always as simple as a discriminatory hiring manager who chooses to give white men more money for the same work as his colleagues. (Although, sometimes this does happen. If that's happened in your company, you should fire that hiring manager.)

Certain work that has stereotypically been seen as "women's work," such as cleaning services or childcare, is frequently compensated at lower rates than "men's work" that requires similar education or training levels, like construction.[39] People of color who did not have access to quality education or elite institutions may not be as highly compensated as a white person with an Ivy League degree, despite their similar work performance.[40] Contracting out for certain jobs—like janitorial staff or food service—has become a common practice, but that also creates lower-paid positions with fewer benefits than a similar in-house job for a full-time employee.[41]

I am not recommending that you pay everyone the same amount as your CEO. But just as you can be innovative when rethinking how you support your frontline employees, you can rethink your compensation structure and policies. The disparity in pay between CEOs and other workers, in particular, has gotten out of control. In 1965, CEOs made 20 times what the typical worker in their industry made. In 2013, that shot up to 296 times.[42] It's no accident that businesses justify this increase as "adding value" at a time when the workforce is diversifying, rather than creating opportunities for more equitable pay.

Maybe you can offer a minimum salary based on the cost of living in your area, or not ask about salary history during the hiring process, so that what you pay isn't based on another company's discriminatory practices. You can also conduct a salary audit of compensation based on gender and race and make it public, to both understand what gaps exist at your company and hold yourself accountable for closing that gap. You can also make it the norm for women and people of color to negotiate their salary and provide them resources to do so—something that most companies don't intentionally do.[43] If you dig into how you make your salary and compensation decisions, I'm sure you'll find something you can change to help create equitable impact.

PUT IT ALL TOGETHER AND CHANGE HOW YOUR COMPANY INVESTS IN YOUR PEOPLE

Table 4.1 is the third iteration of the Good Business Worksheet; it is designed to help you walk through how you invest in your people. As always, you can do this worksheet by yourself or with your team. Again, I've included an agenda (Table 4.2) to help you if you decide to walk it through with your team.

Like the other two, this worksheet distills the lessons presented in this chapter to help you determine which areas of impact are the biggest opportunities for your company. Once you've got those, move to implementation with the Innovate-Accelerate-Decelerate cycle.

TABLE 4.1 Good Business Worksheet, Part 3: How you invest in your people

How you invest in your people

First Step: Understand Your Values Alignment	Innovate	Accelerate	Decelerate
Which areas of impact will help you invest in your people? • Recruitment • Training and Promotion • Compensation • Diversity, Equity, and Inclusion • Benefits • Employee Ownership *What low-hanging fruit that would be easy to change can you identify?* *What higher impact areas can you identify?*	*Which areas of impact within your company can benefit from innovation?* *How will you bring innovative practices into these areas of impact?* *What are your next steps toward implementing these changes across your company?* *Will these changes affect certain groups more than others, and will they worsen or ignore disparities?*	*Which areas of impact can benefit from an acceleration of impact practices?* *How will you accelerate impact practices within these areas of impact?* *What are your next steps toward implementing these changes across your company?* *Will these changes affect certain groups more than others, and will they worsen or ignore disparities?*	*Which areas of impact within your company are doing more harm than good?* *What changes can you make in these areas of impact to decelerate the harm being done?* *What are your next steps toward implementing these changes across your company?* *Will these changes affect certain groups more than others, and will they worsen or ignore disparities?*

TABLE 4.2 Good Business Agenda: How you invest in your people

Time	Topic	Guiding Questions
5 minutes	**Values alignment**	*What are your company values? Do we think we are living those values, or could we do more?* Note: If you don't have company values, spend some time before this meeting creating them as a team.
10 minutes	**Areas of impact**	*In which areas of impact are there opportunities to further invest in the company's employees?* Choose all that are relevant: • Recruitment • Training and Promotion • Compensation • Diversity, Equity, and Inclusion • Benefits • Employee Ownership
15 minutes	**Low-hanging fruit and high impact**	*What are some opportunities where we can easily change things within these areas of impact that will give us quick wins on equitable impact?* *What are some opportunities that will require more time and resources, but will have higher impact long-term?*
25 minutes	**Implementation plan: The Innovate-Accelerate-Decelerate Cycle**	Develop a plan of action by answering the following questions: • *How will you bring innovative practices into these areas of impact?* • *Which areas of impact can benefit from an acceleration of impact practices?* • *Which areas of impact within your company are doing more harm than good?* • *Will these changes affect certain groups more than others, and will they worsen or ignore disparities?*
5 minutes	**Next steps**	*What are your next steps to implementing these changes across your company?*

When to Consider How to Invest in Your People

Just as when you thought about how to make your money, working through the "how to invest in your people" part of the Good Business Worksheet is best done as soon as possible. If you are thinking about hiring your first employee, it is critical to answer these questions *before* you bring someone on. If you've already got a team working with you, you can integrate these questions into a strategic planning conversation or a conversation about staffing and recruitment.

If you don't want to wait that long, integrate these questions into any conversation about benefits, compensation, and recruitment. If you are revisiting your benefits package, consider how you can make changes that are more aligned with your company values. If you are looking to shift up your recruitment approach, use this worksheet to guide you. And, of course, if you have an HR director or an HR team, bring them together and see what they come up with when they walk through this portion of the worksheet.

Steps to Completing the Good Business Worksheet

Step 1: Revisit your company values and consider whether they are still the right ones for the place your company is in right now. It's OK if they aren't—but before you complete this section of the worksheet, you need to come up with values that are authentic to your company and its culture.

Step 2: Now that you have them, think about what those values actually mean. How should your company live those values and create a company culture that reflects those values? Consider which areas of impact are opportunities to better live your values in how you treat your employees:

- Recruitment
- Training and promotion
- Compensation
- Diversity, equity, and inclusion
- Benefits
- Employee ownership

Each of these areas of impact require trade-offs, and some solutions may be more expensive than others. You may need to go back to Chapter 3 and consider how you are spending your money before you can complete this step. Your employees are the most important asset your company has, and investing in them is investing in the success of your company. Determine which trade-offs are worth making to ensure you are fully living your values and creating a thriving, growing corporate culture.

Once you have chosen your top areas for impact, circle them on the worksheet.

Step 3: Think about those low-hanging fruit opportunities once you decided on the top areas of impact. These should be things you can do in the next week or month—maybe reaching out to a community organization to see if you could partner with them on recruiting for an open position. Write these opportunities down underneath the low-hanging fruit question.

Consider next what may be harder, but potentially could deliver more impact: overhauling your compensation practices, or creating an apprenticeship program. Write these under the high-impact question.

Step 4: Now let's move on to the Innovate-Accelerate-Decelerate cycle to begin figuring out how to implement changes in your areas of impact. Start with Innovate and consider which areas would benefit from innovative practices, either coming from within your company, such as adding a new company value of diversity, equity, and inclusion, or outside your company, such as creating better structures to support entry-level workers and reduce turnover. These can be the answers you gave to the low-hanging fruit or high-impact questions, or something else you and your team discussed.

Once you have the areas of impact that can benefit from innovation, write them down on the worksheet. Then, use the remaining questions in the Innovate column to help you figure out how to implement these innovative practices:

- *How will you bring innovative practices into these areas of impact?* Or: What new ideas can help you better invest in your workforce?
- *What are your next steps to implementing these changes across your company?* Or: What needs to get done to allow these changes to happen?
- *Will these changes affect certain groups more than others, and will they worsen or ignore disparities?* Or: Are you missing or not considering potential effects as you think about these new ideas?

Once you have the answers to these questions, write them on the worksheet. Don't forget to actually write them down on the worksheet! That's a critical step that ensures the whole team agrees on what you are committing to.

Step 5: Repeat this process for Accelerate. Can you take something good already happening in your company around one of the areas of impact and expand on it? Or is there something you know others are doing that you want to adopt and grow within your company? Write down in which areas of impact you think you can accelerate some good practices and then answer the following questions to help you agree on next steps:

- *How will you accelerate impact practices within these areas of impact?* Or: What are some good things you are seeing that you can build on to help you invest in your people?
- *What are your next steps to implementing these changes across your company?* Or: How can you support team members to implement these acceleration strategies?
- *Will these changes affect certain groups more than others, and will they worsen or ignore disparities?* Or: More specifically, have you considered how your employees feel or will feel about these changes, as you expand them across the company?

Step 6: Almost done! Do the same thing in the next column for Decelerate. Choose the areas of impact in which you think you need to reduce some harm your company is doing, and answer these questions:

- *What changes can you make in these areas of impact to decelerate the harm being done?* Or: What can you stop doing that would improve your company culture and morale?
- *What are your next steps to implementing these changes across your company?* Or: What steps do you need to take to stop these practices from continuing?
- *Will these changes affect certain groups more than others, and will they worsen or ignore disparities?* Or: Will decelerating these things bring any harm to certain groups? Or could they actually increase disparities?

And make sure you write it all down!

Step 7: Once you're done, make sure everyone agrees on what's written on the worksheet and share it with your team and company. Now all you have to do is get to work on implementing everything you agreed to!

That's it! That's all three components of the Good Business Worksheet. Because this process isn't linear, some of you may be starting here and will go back to the other two components later. That's fine, as long as you make sure you do come back to the steps you skipped. You should start this process wherever it makes sense for your company, but you can't fully do well BY doing good until you've completed the entire worksheet.

Once you have all three worksheets done, you can go back to the summary worksheet in Chapter 1 and fill that out using the information you and your team decided on in Chapters 2 through 4. This version of the worksheet will be a high-level summary, so think of it as a guiding, strategic document rather than an actual action plan. The other worksheets will serve as a supplemental drill down or double click on that overview to help you implement your big picture ideas.

Spotlight On: The Role of Demographics in the Financial Community

Though it may not seem obvious, representation and diversity within the capital markets influences the decision-making of financial firms and the types of businesses they invest in. The demographics of the United States are changing rapidly, and the workforce needs to change with it. So far, this is not happening in most financial institutions.

A study of investment firms with a total of $5.3 trillion in assets under management (AUM) by the Money Management Institute and FundFire found that people of color represented only about 14 percent of managing directors, 23 percent of associates, and 27 percent of analysts. Across all senior levels, people of color represented less than 20 percent of those positions.[44] Similarly, the Knight Foundation found that just 1.3

percent of the almost $70 trillion AUM is managed by women and people of color. Breaking this down a bit more, the Knight Foundation research shows that managers of color manage only 3.9 percent of mutual funds, 8.9 percent of hedge funds, and 1.2 percent of real estate AUM.[45]

Not only are these numbers not representative of the demographics of the population of the United States, they have implications for whose businesses get funded and are able to grow. When looking to make an investment, people tend to choose to invest in a company or person whose characteristics are similar to their own.[46] This means that white, male business leaders automatically are at an advantage walking into any funding or pitch meeting, since those attending likely look like them and have had similar experiences. (These and other barriers to Black business owners were discussed in Chapter 3.)

Diversifying the hiring practices of financial institutions like venture funds, private equity firms, and other asset managers will shift these statistics and put more investment decisions in the hands of people who better represent the changing demographics of America and the world. Increasing diversity alone will not necessarily lead to more equitable funding streams, but it is an important prerequisite. For that to happen, financial institutions will need to adopt practices like those recommended in this chapter to break out of their traditional hiring practices and increase the representation of women and people of color as capital decision makers.

HOW YOU INVEST IN YOUR PEOPLE: SYDNEY'S JEWELRY SHOP

Good news! Sydney's partnership with the nonprofit helped her expand and reach many new customers, which allowed her to hire a local web designer who created a beautiful e-commerce site. Her business is booming! She's at the point now where she can hire her first employee. (What can I say? I raise them right!) Let's see how she'll use the lessons discussed in this chapter to help her with her hiring processes:

Step 1: First, she thinks through her values. No surprise—she goes ahead and adopts my Values Snowball (like mother, like daughter).

Step 2: Sydney's so excited about being able to hire her first employee, she puts all areas of impact on the table. (Go Sydney!)

Step 3: She finds low-hanging fruit for impact in her work environment: (1) a supportive community where her employees feel they can be their full selves and (2) flexibility when needed. Harder to achieve, but higher impact, will be her talent pipeline and training: she wants to exclusively employ people who have either been involved with the justice system or suffered some form of trauma. She wants to give them the skills to not only make and sell her jewelry, but start and run their own businesses.

Step 4: For innovate, she decides to build on her partnership with the girls' empowerment nonprofit, which not only teaches girls how to code but offers financial literacy and entrepreneurship classes to women who need them. She works with the nonprofit to give one of the students hands-on experience as an intern at her company. This both broadens her recruitment pipeline and serves as on-the-job training for the intern.

Step 5: For accelerate, she decides to look into an employee ownership option. If her goal is to help others run their own businesses, bringing employees in as co-owners of the business is a good place to start. They will be even more invested in the company—especially because it is small but growing—and co-ownership gives them more opportunities to be innovative and creative as the company expands. Ideally, she could create different product lines that the employees could own and make theirs.

Step 6: For decelerate, there isn't much since she just started to hire, but she does worry about her ability to recruit and retain a diverse talent pool. The partnership with the nonprofit is a good place to start, but working with a high-needs population can be challenging. She wants to understand more about what as the company's executive she should do to ensure she's supporting those who are helping her company grow.

Step 7: Checking in on her blind spots, Sydney considers any unintended consequences the actions she takes to invest in her people may have. For innovate, she revisits her thinking from Table 2.2, How you make your money worksheet, to ensure that the nonprofit she's partnering with is serving those most in need, and that the intern she currently works with does not have access to internship opportunities elsewhere. For accelerate, she wants to make certain that the co-ownership options she's considering are fair and equitable, she decides to work with an expert to figure out the best way to structure it. For decelerate, she ensures that whatever training or resources she uses include a racial equity lens so that she can learn how to work with everyone in an affirming way.

Step 8: Table 4.3 is Sydney's completed Good Business Worksheet. She hangs it next to the other two, which are now above her

TABLE 4.3 Good Business Worksheet, Part 3: How Sydney's jewelry shop invests in its people

How you invest in your people

First Step: Understand Your Values Alignment	Innovate	Accelerate	Decelerate
Which areas of impact will help you invest in your people? • Recruitment • Training and Promotion • Compensation • Diversity, Equity, and Inclusion • Benefits • Employee Ownership *What is some low-hanging fruit that would be easy to change?* • Offer a flexible, supportive work environment. *What are some areas for higher impact?* • Hire women who have experienced trauma and empower employees to start and grow their own businesses.	*Which areas of impact within your company can benefit from innovation?* • Recruitment/Training and Promotion *How will you bring innovative practices into these areas of impact?* • Create internship with nonprofit. *What are your next steps to implementing these changes across your company?* • Set up a meeting to pitch the proposed internship opportunity. *Will these changes affect certain groups more than others, and will they worsen or ignore disparities?* • Ensure internship is not going to someone with high amount of opportunity.	*Which areas of impact can benefit from an acceleration of impact practices?* • Employee Ownership *How will you accelerate impact practices within these areas of impact?* • Offer employees co-ownership, ideally by allowing them to create their own product lines. *What are your next steps to implementing these changes across your company?* • Look into legal hurdles and structures for this. *Will these changes affect certain groups more than others, and will they worsen or ignore disparities?* • Work with an expert on setting up the structure.	*Which areas of impact within your company are doing more harm than good?* • Diversity, Equity, and Inclusion *What changes can you make in these areas of impact to decelerate the harm being done?* • Understand how to support those who have experienced trauma. *What are your next steps to implementing these changes across your company?* • Identify useful resources and trainings. *Will these changes affect certain groups more than others, and will they worsen or ignore disparities?* • Identify resources with a racial equity approach.

desk in her new office downtown. (Remember, this is hypothetical. I don't let my kids rent office space.) She's ready to keep on growing her business through the power of equitable impact!

Step 9: Every quarter, she meets with her ever-expanding team to revisit these worksheets and see what they can change. She has achieved many of her low-hanging fruit goals, and replaced them with new ones. The Innovate-Accelerate-Decelerate process evolves, as it should, and new areas of impact are tackled. Equitable impact continues to drive her business, and her profits continue to increase along with it!

ADDITIONAL RESOURCES

Examining Your Workforce

The Opportunity Navigator™, a free online tool that companies can use to re-evaluate their hiring practices and help expand their potential workforce, is a collaboration between Talent Rewire and Grads of Life. A community of experts helped define a set of principles and associated talent practices that prioritize equity, inclusion, opportunity, and mobility within your company while generating business value called "Opportunity Employment." The principles include:

- A culture of inclusion and belonging
- A data-driven approach to equity
- Proactive and intentional recruitment
- Minimized barriers to accessing roles
- Family-sustaining wages and benefits for all employees
- Systems that support on-the-job success and ongoing professional development

Their free online diagnostic tool is designed to help get your company started by offering ways in which you can change your hiring practices and help align your HR policies with doing well BY doing good. You can learn more and complete the diagnostic at: https://www.opportunitynavigator.org/

CASE STUDY: EMBEDDING EQUITY: WALMART COMES TO DC

I profiled Walmart's supply chain efforts earlier; now I would like to discuss another aspect of the global corporation's work to embed equitable impact across their company—their recruitment, training, and retention practices, with which I have direct experience.

I started working with Walmart in early 2010 as they were planning their first expansion into the broader Washington, DC, market. This was one of their first tests of "urban" stores; most of their retail locations at that time were in rural, suburban, or exurban markets. They were experiencing challenges expanding into this urban market, which had a different workforce than they were accustomed to. Within the city, the education system was problematic and there was high unemployment. They couldn't recruit talent from outside the city—from the suburbs, for example, because the traffic made it difficult for anyone to travel to work.

One of the things I did to help them solve the problem was to partner with the DC Department of Employment Services, the Community College of the District of Columbia, and other nonprofit and private sector organizations. These partnerships allowed Walmart to expand their recruitment pipeline in the area and gave them access to hire and train the talent they needed to staff their stores.

Part of Walmart's strategy for their market expansion and engagement with a different workforce was to test the effect of a higher wage for their employees. Back then, Walmart had received a lot of criticism for its low wages, which were insufficient for their employees to live on. When it was first announced that Walmart was coming to DC, there was tremendous push-back from the community. There was concern that Walmart would create a "race to the bottom" for retail worker wages.

The DC Council passed a minimum wage bill that was directly targeted at large retailers like Walmart, requiring them to pay a living wage, which at the time was $12.50 an hour. This bill was vetoed by the mayor after Walmart threatened to stop construction on three additional stores, saying they couldn't stay in business with this law in place. The fight left many in the community feeling bitter and wary of Walmart's presence in the city.[47]

After the veto, Walmart continued its expansion into the DC market, but made a commitment to pay a wage that was "at least $1 per hour higher than what is offered currently at Safeway and Giant [local area grocery stores]." In fact, this came to around $12.50 an hour at the time.[48]

After a year operating in the DC market, Walmart hired a firm to analyze their impact on the region. It reported that the two stores that had opened together employed 700 people, 65 percent of whom were DC residents, and were responsible for half of the retail job growth in DC during 2013.[49]

The benefits to the community weren't only related to how Walmart invested in its people. The stores were located in areas identified by the US Department of Agriculture as "food deserts," neighborhoods with no access to fresh foods and vegetables. The Walmart stores brought fresh food to these areas at a low price that people could afford, creating a new revenue stream for the company and offering healthier options for people living in those neighborhoods.[50]

Walmart also affected the community beyond its stores and employees. A separate report by a local DC group found that Walmart hurt other local businesses, whose revenues fell by 20 percent to 85 percent in some cases as they attempted to compete with the giant retailer and its low prices.[51] While Walmart undoubtedly increased job opportunities for those in the local community, it is important for companies to look at the overall net impact of their efforts, particularly when expanding their footprint in a community. A few questions worth reflecting on are: Is your expansion negatively affecting local businesses? Or is it making neighborhoods less affordable due to increased property taxes? Equitable impact extends beyond what's obvious and immediate and companies must be intentional about the ripples of change they create in communities.

Walmart has started a Center for Racial Equity[52] that represents an acknowledgment and approach to move beyond job growth as the sole focus of their impact in their communities. This center focuses on a few issues areas, including finance, health, education, and criminal justice. Through this center, they are working to support Black businesses and other local businesses in communities around the country.

Ultimately, Walmart built six stores in the DC area that were so successful for the company that Walmart decided to expand on the lessons it learned and slowly increased wages in its stores across the country. By 2019 the average hourly wage across the whole company was $13.63.[53]

They did this because it helped their bottom line and also helped their employees. A 2019 report found that in the five years after they began increasing wages, they reduced turnover among their retail employees by 10 percent.[54] In September 2021, facing a labor shortage as a result of the COVID-19 pandemic, Walmart decided to increase its wages by at least $1, which raised the average wage to $16.40; the minimum starting wage went from $11 to $12. In some stores the starting wage was as high as $17 an hour.[55]

Walmart is not a perfect company, and, like all companies, there are certainly things they could be doing differently. That is why there is a "decelerate" section of the Good Business Worksheet. In DC, Walmart attempted to "decelerate" its harmful effects on the small business community by working with local nonprofits and donating to community partnerships that supported job training. But its work to increase its compensation and better support its workforce shows how a company can help improve the lives of its employees while also improving its bottom line.

Walmart's increasing its compensation had a massive impact because of its scale. How could your company have the same impact on its employees, regardless of its size?

5

Build Your CapEQ™ to Make an Equitable Impact

Here we are, getting close to the finish line. Thank you for sticking with it! If you are still reading, you have probably looked through all the resources, completed all the iterations of the Good Business Worksheet, and are excited to start talking with your teams about how to implement what you've learned and harness the full potential of your business.

Before you go skipping off into the sunset and close this book, I want to pull you back a bit and temper your expectations. The resources I've shared so far will help you begin increasing your equitable impact and improving your engagement with your customers, but they are only tools, not guarantees of success. Implementation is harder than filling out worksheets—plans are important—execution is the real challenge.

The truth is, you will probably face resistance to some of your equitable impact strategies. If you are a junior staff member, the leadership of your company may not be on board immediately, no matter how well-crafted your proposals are. If you are the boss, some of your staff may pay lip service to these ideas, but not commit fully to their execution. You may struggle to find the right partners to help implement your process; you may have some quick early wins, only to struggle and lose focus after a few months executing on your strategies. I've seen it all before—the path isn't linear, and can be frustrating.

Don't worry, I'm not going to leave you without any support as you start your doing well BY doing good journey. The way that you mitigate these ongoing challenges to implementing the plans you developed using the Good Business Worksheet is by increasing your company's overall *capacity* to do this type of work. Plans are great, but if you are running a business, you know that success comes from more than just good planning. You need a strong, competent team with the right skills and knowledge to be able to execute on those plans, test them out, and see what works.

Building this skill set in your company may require a culture shift or a reorientation of your company's purpose. Maybe your company has primarily been motivated or driven by profit margins without regard to its effect on all stakeholders; if so, you'll have to ease off that for a bit in order for these changes to take hold to create your desired longer-term impact. Maybe you have a very established hiring process and culture onboarding process; that may need to shift. Your team may have to alter their focus, if only slightly, to acquire new knowledge and put their energy into different things.

But if you can make these cultural shifts and strengthen the resiliency and capacity of your organization, implementation will be easier. This cultural reorientation is big and will take time, but it will make your company stronger. You will be able to benefit not only from what you have built with your business to date, but you will expand on that success to acquire a new customer base with deeper engagement.

As I've said throughout this book, you should start this process wherever you think is right for you, your team, and your business. It may be with how you invest in your people, or it could be with a very specific procurement request for proposal (RFP) you have coming out next week. Starting somewhere is better than starting nowhere—as long as your goal is embedding equitable impact everywhere.

However, If you want to go deeper into what it takes to truly leverage the benefits of equitable impact with your customers, I will now walk you through a series of resources that can strengthen your company's ability to do well BY doing good, not just instructions on how to put a plan together to change a product line or create a new community partnership.

I developed the CapEQ™ Continuum to help businesses walk through a step-by-step process for increasing their capacity to create equitable impact while expanding their profits. You can think of the capacity-building efforts as a parallel track to the advice I presented in earlier chapters. Usually, I recommend that my clients pursue both tracks at the same time: what they develop through the Good Business Worksheet can be thought of as an initial pilot program to test out immediate opportunities for equitable impact. The capacity-building work occurs throughout these pilots, and when the business is able to pick all their low-hanging fruits, they have the ability to take on more costly, but higher-impact projects.

CAPITALISM + EQUITABLE IMPACT

You've probably heard of IQ, that supposed universal test of intelligence. You may have even heard of EQ, which measures someone's aptitude for emotional intelligence. But have you heard of *CapEQ?*

CapEQ™ is not only the name of my firm, it's a concept I developed to help you and your company understand your capacity and willingness to do well BY doing good. It's what happens when you use the tools of capitalism to create equitable impact.

We need to add equitable impact to capitalism because, although the engine of American capitalism has been proven to be a wealth generator, it has also proven to be a disparity generator. Despite all the inequities that capitalism creates, working within the capitalist system offers great potential in order to achieve the promise of the American ideals of freedom, mobility, and opportunity for all. It's just hard to do—as almost 250 years of disparity and inequality have taught us.

During the Gilded Age of US history there were challenges to democracy—voter fraud, monopolies, and other forms of corruption and intimidation. The more wealth people amassed, the more they worked to keep it for themselves at the expense of others, even if it meant rigging the fight in their favor. As a result, income inequality skyrocketed to untenable levels. Labor, which produced the goods and services, was not earning wages commensurate with the value they created, not too different from when our country was founded and our national wealth was amassed through slave labor.

As a result of the disparities of the Gilded Age, the United States built guardrails around its capitalist system through a series of policies that protected workers by standardizing working conditions, limiting the total number of hours in the workweek, setting a minimum wage, and introducing other reforms. These policies were an attempt to begin defining and refining the ideals of American capitalism, and brought us back closer to the ultimate promise of capitalism: Hard work should pay off. Competition should be fair. And aligned incentives should yield mutual benefit for the employee, the consumer, and the company.

Our capitalist system has not always lived up to these ideals. The 2008 financial crisis showed us what happens when the guardrails come off and a small group of powerful decision-makers have free rein to do whatever they want with the markets. The fallout from the COVID-19 pandemic illustrated how frontline workers don't get the protections or support they need, whereas wealthier "knowledge workers" were permitted to work from home and, therefore, protect themselves and their families.

Despite these warranted critiques of how capitalism has functioned in the United States, we still have the opportunity to make capitalism work as it was intended. That is why I am so dedicated to the capitalist model and capitalist ideals. The beauty of the system is that when capitalism functions well it should result in mutual benefit, that holy trinity of capitalism I discussed in Chapter 1. The idea that we can work together to better ourselves and others in fair and competitive trade is still worth fighting for.

Capitalism has had its failings, but by intentionally addressing the inequities in the system, we can make it a powerful tool for change. We need to combine the principles of capitalism with the strength of equitable impact to ensure that we are operating in a way that aligns with the promise of capitalism— that we can create mutual benefit for everyone.

This is the reasoning behind CapEQ. Fundamentally, your CapEQ measures you and your company's willingness to rebuild capitalism and to simultaneously be driven by the values and culture of equitable impact. Bringing an equitable approach to capitalism allows you to see the human impact of your company, not just the financial impact, and helps you understand how the results of your business affect people and communities in unintended ways.

THE CapEQ™ CONTINUUM

The CapEQ continuum was developed by me and my team after working with hundreds of companies, nonprofits, and government agencies to help them create financial and social value. It is a simple, easy way for you and your company to determine what areas within your company need investment so you can successfully execute on the plans you created using the Good Business Worksheets. It evaluates your company's practices based on a series of elements and places your company on a continuum from high CapEQ to low CapEQ. Improving your capacity in those areas can move your company from a low CapEQ to a high CapEQ.

There are five elements to CapEQ: buy-in, knowledge, quick wins, resources, and business model.

Buy-In

If you are reading this and you are the boss, then good work! You've already gotten buy-in—or you are on a good path to do so.

For the rest of my readers, the major gating factor to being able to implement new strategies for equitable impact is whether or not senior leadership has bought into the concept of doing well BY doing good. Nothing stands in your way like a boss who isn't interested in what you are selling. Such resistance can be subtle—they are all smiles in meetings, but there's no follow-up—or it can be explicit: a door slammed in your face! (Maybe not literally. . . .)

You may face resistance, as some business leaders hold fast to the mantra of "the business of business is business." They do not want anything to do with something they see as irrelevant to their business model. Or, and this can be even worse, they already think they are doing enough through their corporate philanthropy or company volunteer program. They don't want to push themselves to do more than the bare minimum.

Unfortunately, without buy-in at the top of the company, or at least in critical departments, it's unlikely that you'll be able to implement much of my recommendations. All is not lost, because a critical part of increasing a company's CapEQ is to make the case for why the company needs to integrate equitable impact into their operations.

Securing this buy-in is similar to any change management activity you've completed at your company—whether it's rolling out a new HRIS system or onboarding a new CEO. You should first identify your problem areas (or people) as well as your areas of strength. If there are a few people at the company really passionate about this work, create an informal team and strategize how you can get more buy-in from the top. You can figure out a pilot opportunity; that's a type of low-hanging fruit you develop using the Good Business Worksheet, and generate some quick wins to illustrate potential. You can also share some of the information and trends we've discussed to demonstrate the need to take on social causes in order for your company to remain competitive.

The remaining elements of the continuum can help you with the buy-in process. If you know that building capacity in one area would support this change management process, dive in and go from there!

Knowledge

Central to a strong CapEQ is staff knowledge on how to do well BY doing good. This is an easy fix—just give everyone at your company this book! If you are reading this, you've acquired enough knowledge to be considered the resident expert.[1]

If making your whole company read this book isn't feasible, you can share individual resources that I've highlighted in Chapters 2, 3, and 4 that you think might resonate with your coworkers or employees. Just as you need your staff to have a basic understanding of the ins and outs of your industry, it's important that everyone on the team has a shared understanding of *why* you are making these changes to your company and how they will lead to greater impact for your community and your profits. This foundational knowledge will set your company up for success in the long run.

Increasing capacity in this area isn't tricky—it just takes commitment. Study, study, study!

Quick Wins

Knowing something isn't the same thing as doing something. To increase your CapEQ, your company has to demonstrate its ability to create equitable impact. What are the things you can change in your company to show that doing well BY doing good is possible?

When I work with clients, usually they have no idea how to start integrating equitable impact into their operations. But a few small changes and some evidence of success are enough to show what is possible and create momentum inside the company. It also helps to balance a sense of urgency to take action with the reality that long-term cultural shifts within a company take time and investment.

Small wins will lead to further success and build a foundation for future work. This is where that low-hanging fruit comes in and why it is so important. Determining where easy solutions can be implemented will help to show your staff and leadership what is possible and create the goodwill to move further up the CapEQ continuum.

As you build capacity in the other elements, these quick wins will turn into sustainable shifts within the organization. You'll develop systems and infrastructure to support equitable impact across your company. Combining the lessons learned from these wins with the resources to grow your impact will help change your business model to maximize the full potential of your company.

Resources

If a business wants to do anything, it needs the money and resources to do it. Before setting off, it's important that your company sets aside resources for equitable impact or social engagement. Without adequate resources committed to this process, it will be hard for your company to successfully implement all of the solutions identified by the Good Business Worksheet.

This may also seem like a pretty straightforward capacity area—either you have dedicated resources for equitable impact or you don't. But actually, it's not that simple. Many companies will start an "office of impact" or assign one staff member to coordinate involvement with social causes. There's nothing wrong with approaching your resourcing of equitable impact in that way, but it can create a "siloed" effect. Remember, equitable impact should be a main course, not a side dish, and setting up a small "team of impact" may have that effect.

If you do have dedicated staff, make sure they are seen as facilitators or as a support team that's coordinating activity across the company. If you are resourcing the work across the company, you can assign a point person to be the lead for that team or department and encourage coordination among these individuals.

Essentially, you cannot expect to be able to implement your good business plans unless you recognize implementation takes time and money. Once you've identified the changes you want to make, ensure that your staff or team members have the resources they need to execute on those plans, in whatever way they need to do so.

Business Model

If you want to make equitable impact your company's main course, you'll have to understand how your core business model aligns with the equitable impact you want to create. To have the highest CapEQ possible, your business should operate in a way that creates equitable impact whenever you bring in revenue or make a profit.

This may be the hardest area to change within your company, and it requires strong capacity in the other CapEQ areas. Some companies can easily shift their business model to align with equitable impact, but for some it's much harder. Greyston Bakery, discussed in Chapter 4, has a very clear, socially-aligned business model. They say, "We don't hire people to bake brownies, we bake brownies to hire people."[2] For others, like Doc-Scan (see Chapter 2), changing a business model may be uncomfortable or may not always be feasible, at least not then.

To truly do well BY doing good, your company's purpose—its business model—must be fully aligned with the equitable impact you want to create. Doing this will take all of the other elements of the CapEQ continuum:

- Buy-in from senior leadership to begin and continue the process
- The knowledge of what it takes to create equitable impact
- Quick wins to demonstrate success and build momentum
- The resources to keep everything going

All of these combine to shift your business model and create a company that exists to create social and financial returns.

This of course takes time and energy. It won't happen overnight. But many companies have developed a business model that combines the financial and the social—you can too.

WHAT'S YOUR CapEQ?

Now that you know these elements, let's figure where your company fits on the CapEQ continuum. The five elements of the continuum track to the five levels of impact readiness (see Figure 5.1). Because this is a continuum, there's a spectrum of possibilities for where your company fits; most companies move from one level to the next as they increase their CapEQ.

	LEVEL 1	LEVEL 2	LEVEL 3	LEVEL 4	LEVEL 5
BUY-IN Buy-in and support at executive level	X	✓	✓	✓	✓
KNOWLEDGE Internal capabilities or talent with skills and know-how	X	X	✓	✓	✓
QUICK WINS Demonstration of success	X	? Activities, no infrastructure	? Strong activities, some infrastructure	✓	✓
RESOURCES Financial and talent resources to activate impact	X	X	X	?	✓
BUSINESS MODEL Authentic model conducive to optimized impact	X	?	?	?	✓

FIGURE 5.1 The five levels of impact readiness on the CapEQ Continuum

Below are some guidelines that will help you determine where your company is on the continuum:

Level 1: You are here if you have not progressed in any of these areas—no buy-in, no activities to support equitable impact, no internal knowledge about what it takes, no dedicated resources—and your business model does not contain any equitable impact element. If your company is at Level 1, don't worry. Let's keep moving up the continuum to see how you can improve.

Level 2: At this level, you are just starting the process. You have buy-in across your company, or at least from your leadership, but you don't have much more than that. You may have a few quick wins, but they are recent, and equitable impact has not yet been integrated beyond these few activities.

Level 3: Now your staff has the knowledge to implement innovative equitable impact strategies, which means your activities are stronger and you are developing some established infrastructure for equitable impact.

Level 4: To reach this level means you have started to dedicate resources to equitable impact, but mostly in the form of staff. To get to the next level, you'll need to rethink your business model to bring in a dedicated income stream that connects to your equitable impact goals.

Level 5: You've made it! You are firing on all cylinders. You've successfully built capacity in all areas, allowing you to create a business model that helps you impact your main course. You are fully equipped to execute on all elements of the Good Business Worksheet.

THE SECRETS OF BUILDING YOUR CapEQ

Let's take another step deeper into the CapEQ continuum and how you can use it to strengthen your company's capacity for equitable impact. As I said at the beginning of the chapter, building your CapEQ requires making some fundamental cultural shifts within your company. Because your company culture is made up of individuals, there are some things you and your employees will have to grapple with to help orient everyone toward a more equitable capitalism.

We all have been taught or learned things about how our society works, which influence how we behave and what we think about the world. Some of these things are good and useful, and can help you survive, for example, treating others like you want to be treated, working hard and following through on your commitments, and telling the truth

But there are other things we are taught that may not be true, or may not be the whole truth. These may be prejudices or biases, but they can also be mental models for how we think about the world. One example I referenced earlier is that businesses should focus only on making profits and nothing else. We know now that isn't true, but for a while it was considered gospel (and some people still think it is!). You also may have been taught that people who work hard succeed, and if someone isn't successful, or lives in poverty, it's because they haven't worked hard enough. Walk into any fast-food restaurant or other place where people work (often at multiple jobs) for minimum wage and tell me they aren't working hard—or even harder—than someone who has an easier job for better pay.

As you implement your plans using the Good Business Worksheet and build up your CapEQ capacity, you may run into coworkers who believe these learned mental models, which can make it hard for you to move forward with implementing equitable impact strategies. Or there may be people in your company who hold mental models that make them resist working differently. This makes it harder to secure buy-in and integrate equitable impact throughout your company.

Challenging these beliefs is normal and a part of the process. I have seen this happen time and time again. That's why the real secret to building your CapEQ is to confront these beliefs in yourself and others and work to shift mindsets to be more open to what doing well BY doing good can do for you, your company, and society.

I have identified three of the major mental models that limit a company's CapEQ. Shifting these mindsets can help you and your company rethink how you do business and create value.

Mindset: Winner Take All

The first shift to help you build your CapEQ is to move from a place of scarcity to a place of abundance. You often hear phrases like "dog-eat-dog" or "zero-sum game" with respect to the business ecosystem, which makes it seem like an over-competitive, I-win-you-lose atmosphere. That's because, for the most part, we operate in a society that is zero-sum and relies on a framework of scarcity.

But it doesn't have to be that way. Approaching things from a scarcity mindset—whether that's thinking about your quarterly sales, your supply chain, or something as large scale as the global economic market—will only limit you in what you want to achieve. Shifting to a mindset of abundance can help you realize the many resources you have at your disposal to create the impact you want to see.

At the project management software company Basecamp, for example, employees work no more than 32 hours a week.[3] Its CEO isn't impressed by staff who work overtime, and celebrates that his employees have abundant, full lives. Yet they are still able to maintain thousands of customers.[4] How?

Instead of thinking of their time as a scarce resource, the company prioritizes treating their employees right. And by limiting work hours to allow staff to invest in other parts of their lives, the company is able to prioritize the things that matter. They have shifted their mindset around what it means to work hard and have found that there are enough resources for employees to both be successful at work and live full lives.

To shift this mindset in you and your company, consider your true strengths and the strengths of your network, and how you can nurture your network while also growing your company. There may be customers you never considered before, or a talent pool you never tapped into because you were focused too much on limits and not enough on potential.

Mindset: The Great Man Theory of Success

We all know the story—the exceptional founder starting a company in his (it's almost always a "he") basement, working at it for years, and turning that company into a multibillion-dollar enterprise. This heroic story doesn't only apply to businesses. We remember presidents or other public figures as great men who turned the tide of history, and forget the social movements that led to and supported the changes ushered in by these individuals.

But most of us also know that the heroic story isn't the full story. That individual founder had a team behind him, and presidents have their cabinets, supporters, and grassroots volunteers. No one ever really does anything alone.

Companies are beginning to understand the power of community in their consumer base. Many are nurturing "brand ambassadors"—customers who love their products and want to support the mission of the company. Athleta, the fitness wear company referenced in Chapter 2, has developed a network of Athleta Ambassadors[5] to spread the word about their products and live its mission of empowering women. Relying heavily on social media, these ambassadors form a community to expand Athleta's customer base beyond what the company could do on its own.

Consider how you understand and authentically connect with your community to identify your unique value proposition. By figuring out what your customers want from you, you can begin to invest in and grow an interconnected community that thrives together. You will be surprised what you'll find when you look beyond the individual and see the community support that exists for those that need it.

Mindset: Survival of the Fittest

Thinking in abundance and building a community requires a collaborative mindset, different from the competitive approach most businesses take. I'm not saying that you should drop all elements of competition—that's what allows capitalism to thrive, after all. But a collaborative approach can help you see where your strengths complement the other company's weaknesses, and how you could both grow together in a sustainable way. For this reason, I refer to CapEQ's clients as partners; we are building a collaborative network of companies and organizations committed to doing well BY doing good.

One of the first things I ask my clients when working with them is: Who is your competition? Is it another company with a similar business model? Or is there some systemic issue that you want to eliminate from the market that will help everyone?

Take the example of Griffin Hospital, an acute care hospital in Connecticut. In the 1980s, they were known as a hospital to avoid. Today, they are an award-winning, patient-centered hospital with great results.[6] How did they make this shift? Well, when the CEO decided they needed to make a change, instead of focusing on growth that took clients away from another hospital, they focused on something bigger: the entire way of doing business in the healthcare industry. They focused on building community with staff, patients, and volunteers, and developed a culture that helped them thrive.

When you set your sights on solving a problem that is bigger than an industry or market, you can collaborate effectively with others. Making this competitive/collaborative mindset shift can help you see your business model in a whole new way and fundamentally change how your business does business.

THE ULTIMATE GOAL: CHANGING SYSTEMS

The CapEQ Continuum helps increase your company's capacity to do well BY doing good, and the Good Business Worksheet helps you implement your solutions and plans to harness the power of equitable impact to secure new customers and strengthen your relationship with them. If you commit to these processes and dedicate the right amount of resources and time to them, you can transform your business to become a company that is fully aligned with equitable impact. There is no difference between your ability to generate profit and your ability to generate equitable impact. You can become a company that is fully equipped for the opportunities of the modern business climate.

If you undergo this transformation, you will be undertaking what academics and researchers call "systems change." This is a hard concept to grasp, but it is a critical concept for the creation of equitable impact, whether at the company level or the societal level.

The great systems thinker Donella Meadows describes a system as "an interconnected set of elements that is coherently organized in a way that achieves something."[7] This is a simple definition of a complex idea. Systems are all around us—we have an educational system that teaches our children, a criminal justice system that punishes people who break the laws we have agreed to, a financial system that distributes money across our economy, and an agricultural system that produces food for us to eat. Systems don't have to be social or require human intervention: there are environmental systems like the water cycle, weather patterns, and ocean ecosystems.

Talking about systems is so challenging because, as individuals, we don't really see them. We just live our lives, and the systems produce the outcomes we want. Our kids go to school, traffic flows on the highway, the lights turn on when we flip a switch. The problem arises when the systems we don't really see produce outcomes that aren't great. Black men go to jail way more frequently than white men, income inequality skyrockets, our world gets hotter and hotter.

Because we don't see these systems, it is much harder to change them when we want to. John Kania, Mark Kramer, and Peter Senge wrote a report called "The Water of Systems Change" for FSG, the social impact consulting firm. They tell a variation of a story that's commonly used to discuss systems and systems change:

> A fish is swimming along one day when another fish comes up and says "Hey, how's the water?" The first fish stares back blankly at the second fish and then says "What's water?"[8]

How are we expected to change the water all around us if we can't even see it? Luckily, systems experts have been thinking about this problem for decades and have some suggestions. Kania, Kramer, and Senge distill some of the major lessons of systems thinking and the experts who study systems to come up with what they call the Six Conditions of Systems Change (see Figure 5.2).

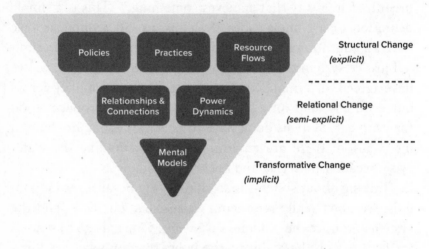

FIGURE 5.2 Six conditions of systems change[9]

The authors define each condition as follows:

1. **Policies:** Government, institutional, and organizational rules, regulations, and priorities that guide the entity's own and others' actions.
2. **Practices:** Espoused activities of institutions, coalitions, networks, and other entities targeted to improving social and environmental progress. Also, within the entity, the procedures, guidelines, or informal shared habits that comprise their work.
3. **Resource Flows:** How money, people, knowledge, information, and other assets such as infrastructure are allocated and distributed.

4. **Relationships & Connections:** Quality of connections and communication occurring among actors in the system, especially among those with differing histories and viewpoints.

5. **Power Dynamics:** The distribution of decision-making power, authority, and both formal and informal influence among individuals and organizations.

6. **Mental Models:** Habits of thought—deeply held beliefs and assumptions and taken-for-granted ways of operating that influence how we think, what we do, and how we talk.[10]

These six conditions all have effects from the explicit to the implicit. While explicit changes are the easiest to see, they actually have the smallest impact. The more implicit changes are, the more long-term impact they can have.

The first three conditions—policies, practices, and resource flows—all produce explicit, structural changes. Kania, Kramer, and Senge use the example of the Affordable Care Act as an example of these kinds of explicit system change. The ACA changed policies around healthcare; for example, insurance companies were no longer able to deny coverage based on pre-existing health conditions. It also changed healthcare practices, such as incentivizing preventive care. The ACA also expanded access to insurance, which was a massive change in resource flows for the economy. But while it delivered these tangible benefits, it didn't really change Americans' mindset around healthcare as a fundamental human right (at least not initially), and it received strong resistance from conservatives who saw it as government overreach.

Relational changes are semi-explicit, and can produce tangible and intangible results. These are changes in relationships or power dynamics that can lead to explicit changes. The authors reference an antihomelessness initiative in Los Angeles that led to new connections between the city government and county government that had never before worked together, despite each overseeing elements of the system that provides services for individuals without a home. The two governments were able to agree on joint funding of new housing units that would help reduce homelessness—something that wouldn't have happened without the change in relationships.

The final type of system change condition—mental models—is the most powerful and can lead to true transformational change. But this type of change is also the most implicit, hardest to see, and hardest to achieve. These are the changes to our way of thinking that help us rethink things we have been taught or assumptions we hold that are no longer helpful. Changes to our mental models can have dramatic and lasting impact, even if those changes come over time and it's hard to draw a connection from one to the next.

Kania, Kramer, and Senge use the example of the Mothers Against Drunk Driving campaign that changed people's mental model about drunk driving by showing the impact of losing a child to such an accident. This campaign shifted drunk driving from a tolerable and common issue to something inexcusable and immoral, undoubtedly saving thousands of lives. Changes in our perceptions about smoking is another example of a transformative mental model change. Even things like changing perceptions of gender norms or race relations are mental model shifts, and show how powerfully the way we think about the world can influence people's lives and how we act as a society.

CHANGE YOUR BUSINESS, CHANGE YOUR SYSTEM

What does all this system change stuff mean for your business? It means that no matter the size of your company, you can be a part of large-scale changes to our society. By following the steps outlined in this book, you can help influence all of the six conditions of systems change. Each of the ways you change your business practices—how you make your money, how you spend your money, and how you invest in your people—can change the bigger systems you operate in.

Changing your practices so your product development is carbon neutral will have a direct impact on reducing greenhouse gases and improving our environmental system. Creating new relationships with local businesses to diversify your procurement contracts can help those businesses grow and thrive, reinvesting even more back into the community. Rethinking your hiring practices and where you go to source talent can create a mental model shift in your company about who might be a good employee and why. And, if you work in partnership with other businesses around all of these changes—taking that mindset shift from competition to collaboration—changes within your business can lead other companies to do the same.

As you revisit the Good Business Worksheet and work to implement the recommendations, consider which systems you want to change and how your solutions will influence each of the six conditions of systems change. The environment may be most important to you, or perhaps it's the criminal justice system. Maybe changing the educational system aligns more with your business model. Ultimately, the Good Business Worksheet and the CapEQ Continuum aren't just about increasing your capacity as a company, but increasing our ability as a society to use capitalism as a tool to create prosperity for all.

I have decided the system I want to change is how the world does business. It is my life's goal. It has brought me to all kinds of clients working to do different things. (It also brought me to writing this book.) It is a big goal, and a big system to change, but we can do it if we all work together and leverage the true potential of business. Thank you for joining me on this journey and working to do well BY doing good.

CapEQ QUIZ

Does your company have a mission statement or similar statement that includes a commitment to equitable impact?

1. No written mission statement
2. Yes, a mission statement with stated values related to equitable impact (i.e., diversity, inclusion, etc.)
3. Yes, a mission statement with stated equitable impact areas of focus (i.e., environment, human rights, etc.)
4. Yes, a mission statement with specific equitable impact goals (i.e., increasing affordable housing, reducing waste, etc.)

Does your company have professional development or other training for staff around concepts related to equitable impact?

1. No.
2. No, but staff are interested in the topic and some do independent learning.
3. Yes, we have one professional development or educational resource for staff around equitable impact.
4. Yes, we have multiple resources for staff to support their learning around equitable impact.

How many initiatives (internal or external) has your company implemented around equitable impact?

1. None
2. 1–2
3. 3–5
4. Everything our business does is connected to equitable impact in some way.

Does your company have staff dedicated to equitable impact?

1. No dedicated staff
2. Staff with some portion of their responsibility related to equitable impact
3. One staff person who is completely dedicated to equitable impact
4. 2+ staff members who are completed dedicated to equitable impact

What are your motivations for pursuing equitable impact through your company (please choose the primary motivator)?

1. Competitive pressure to focus more on equitable impact, either from customers, staff, or other market elements
2. A desire to do good for the world
3. To help develop innovative new products or processes
4. It is a part of the core business model

Total up all numbers associated with your answer: _____

Levels associated with your score:

> **Level 1:** 4
> **Level 2:** 5–8
> **Level 3:** 9–12
> **Level 4:** 13–18
> **Level 5:** 19–20

CONCLUSION

Changing How YOU Do Business

I began my career before everyone had a cellphone or an email address. I didn't own a computer, and, at the office, I worked at a big, clunky desktop. Many of my bosses and higher-ups didn't use computers, even though I was working for the industrial giant, GE, within its "eBusiness" division. Computers and the internet were so new that some departments used the internet; others did not.

Back then, an "e" business was shorthand for something innovative. It signaled a changing economy and a whole new way to sell products and make money. eBusiness and e-commerce were the hot new thing, with seemingly limitless potential and opportunity for business growth. Investors couldn't get enough of these online business models.

We learned pretty quickly thanks to the dot-com bust that sticking an "e" before your name or a ".com" after didn't guarantee your company massive revenue or customers. The promises of companies like Pets.com or eToys.com proved to be a little shortsighted and short-lived. Jobs were lost, and millions of dollars of value evaporated overnight.

But while Pets.com is no more, other early pioneers of e-commerce are still with us. Companies like Amazon and Netflix pivoted and grew after the dot-com bubble burst and are now among the biggest corporations in the world. They have redefined their industries. And, of course, companies like Twitter, Google, Facebook, Apple, and YouTube used the infrastructure created by the internet to create new industries, new products, and new services.

I haven't worked for GE in a while, but I would make a safe bet that there is no part of that company that doesn't use the internet in some way. Even though all of the "e" products and service lines didn't necessarily work out, technology and the internet completely changed how that company did business.

If you visit the GE website now, you won't find anything with "e" in front of it. Yes, it does have a digital division that develops business software, but gone are the days of GE hiring young, ambitious people as e-business analysts. (If you try to google "GE eBusiness jobs," it autocorrects to "GE Business jobs.") They've dropped the "e," and now they just are doing business.

I am sure I am not the first person to point out to you how much the internet and technology has changed our lives. We all have a computer in our pocket more powerful than any piece of hardware I could have worked with in my first job at GE. You may be reading this on your phone or tablet—something inconceivable just a few years ago.

What is also remarkable is how this shift happened at companies like GE and others. They didn't have a big meeting one day to announce they were removing the "e" from their job titles and that the internet would now be a part of every product line and business area. It just happened—quietly, part of the processes and operations of influential people who made decisions in the best interests of the company. Of course, it seems obvious now that technology would drive all of our business operations, but it wasn't back then. There was still a lot to figure out, and a lot of mistakes to be made. We did figure it out, and then some, bringing innovation to our work and using technologies in new and different ways. You probably didn't know these changes were happening at GE and other companies (unless you worked there), but they were. Now, here we are.

We are at the same place right now with business and equitable impact as we were with technology and business in the late 1990s. Companies are increasingly recognizing the need to integrate equitable impact into their operations, but they don't know how. Mistakes are being made. Innovative ideas are being developed. We're creating offices of social impact and product lines designed with equitable impact in mind, separate from our other business processes.

Soon, though, the companies successfully integrating equitable impact into their work will distinguish themselves from those that can't figure it out, and customers and the markets will reward them for doing so. The nature and definition of what "business" means will shift once again—instead of referring to things as a "social enterprise" or an "impact investment" or a "business for good," we'll drop the modifiers and doing well BY doing good will just be how business gets done. There won't be a big meeting to discuss it, just the shifting expectations and practices of people across companies making the decisions to maximize the full potential of their businesses.

To be a part of this change, and not be left behind, you can change your business practices in three areas:

1. **How you make your money:** Changing your business model can help put equitable impact at the core of your operations.
2. **How you spend your money:** Thinking about how your company spending is affecting the community around you can help create a stronger work culture and signal your values to customers.
3. **How you invest in your people:** Seeing your employees and potential employees as assets to invest in can help reduce your turnover, increase productivity, and make a meaningful difference in the lives of those who help you achieve your business goals.

If you are successful in implementing the lessons from this book, your customers may never know about the intentional process you went through to make these organizational shifts. But, like a real estate developer who saw what a building could become just by looking at a blueprint, you and your team will be able to experience these changes with pride knowing together you saw the building before others even knew you could break ground.

My lifelong goal is to change how the world does business. This book is about how to change how you do business. Do not fall behind the trends that are forcing companies to take equitable impact seriously, but also don't be too bold and overpromise—you don't want to be the Pets.com of equitable impact. Use the lessons in this book to intentionally, authentically change your company so that you can do well BY doing good in a way that makes sense for you, your employees, your customers, and all your stakeholders.

If you do, I know we can achieve this moonshot together.

Don't forget—more insights and resources to help are available for free at CapEQimpact.com.

ACKNOWLEDGMENTS

While I was writing this book, my grandma passed away on November 21, less than a month before her 102nd birthday. She has always been the smartest person I've ever known, but my lens of her was limited to the role she played in my life. As I read her obituary, I was struck by how much impact she had had on the world around her. Although they were US citizens, Grandma Boyea and her family were unjustly incarcerated at Manzanar, a concentration camp located in the desolate California desert, during World War II. At Manzanar, Grandma taught students, established the library, and led the initiative to successfully place student internees at prominent colleges on the East Coast, even petitioning the president of the United States to demand justice for her people. Even before NASA, it is clear I inherited my moonshot mindset from her, and I am so grateful for her vision and example.

Despite my moonshot mindset, it is still frightening to put vision on paper, and everyone needs a group of people who love you enough to tell you what works, what doesn't, and why about what you're sharing. Immense gratitude to John King (my mentor), Casey Recupero (my brother), and Demetria Silvera (my sister) for their willingness to read my raw drafts with care and consideration. Your insights and recommendations made the book stronger and made me more confident that I had something worth sharing. Similarly, I'm grateful for Jay

Coen Gilbert for lending his voice and support to the foreword. He is a pioneer in this space, and, I am humbled and honored that he would amplify my work.

At CapEQ our clients are our partners, and so many of these stories are possible because of the partnership with people who were willing to pioneer these practices before they were popular. A few of these partners are: Mahlet Getachew, PolicyLink; Lissa Glasgo, Global Impact Investing Network; Michelle Gilliard, formerly of Walmart; Nick Jean-Baptiste from Jacmel Growth Partners; Ashleigh Gardere, formerly of the NOLABA; Nicole Trimble, formerly of Talent Re-Wire; Greg Tomlins, Caterpillar; Bridgette Corridan, Athleta; Stephanie Ryan, B Lab; Ted, Ned, and Rooney Castle, Rhino Foods; Fay Hanleybrown, FSG; and Kevin Eppler, White Men for Racial Justice.

When McGraw Hill agreed to publish this book, we were incredibly giddy! Thanks to our original editor and our current team, Amy Li, Jonathan Sperling, and Donya Dickerson. And we wouldn't have even met with McGraw Hill if John Coleman, author of *HBR Guide to Crafting Your Purpose,* among others, hadn't graciously connected us to his publisher who facilitated the introduction. And somewhere in my youth or childhood I must have done something good, because I could not have written this book or many of my musings without the brilliance and support of Jeff Raderstrong.

Speaking of brilliance and support—those words encompass the team at CapEQ! There are so many avengers who have worked with us at different stages of this journey, and I'm eternally grateful for everything you have brought individually and collectively. Tracey Jarmon, I can't thank you enough for your sprinkles, vision, and support.

No one gets to where they are without family, and I'm grateful for the discipline, faith, and optimism instilled by my parents Bruce, Dee Dee, and Suzette, and for the joy and laughter I can always find in the homes and hearts of my sisters

Tiki and Nychi. I have been especially moved by my sister Keil as she brings her intelligence and activism in corporate spaces—Anson would be so proud of you and grateful for our relationship. And who could ask for better examples than my two sisters, world-renowned author Monica West and entrepreneur extraordinaire Marlissa Hudson. They push me to be the best version of myself; I hit the life lotto when Providence brought us together.

Most importantly, ultimate thanks go to Dylan, Sydney, and Keith. To Sydlan—I had so much fun sharing glimpses of how each of you are growing into fully formed humans who will consider the steps outlined in this book just the way business is done. And Keith, your love and partnership creates the space for this and so much more.

Lastly, thanks to you, dear reader. The only way we can change how the world does business is together. Leaders like you sustain my hope that this is possible, and I hope we continue to partner together on this path to just change.

NOTES

INTRODUCTION

1. Whittaker, Martin, and Peter Georgescu. "Don't believe the cynics: Done right, stakeholder capitalism is what America needs." *Fortune*, August 18, 2017. https://fortune.com/2021/08/18/stakeholder -capitalism-business-roundtable-corporate-purpose-just-capital/.
2. Nielsen. "The Global, Socially-Conscious Consumer." March 2012. https://www.nielsen.com/us/en/insights/report/2012/the-global— socially-conscious-consumer/.
3. Maheshwari, Sapna. "Revealed: The People Behind an Anti-Breitbart Twitter Account." *New York Times*. July 20, 2018. https:// www.nytimes.com/2018/07/20/business/media/sleeping-giants -breitbart-twitter.html.
4. Gilbert, Jay. "The Millennials: A new generation of employees, a new set of engagement policies." *Ivery Business Journal*. September/ October 2011. https://iveybusinessjournal.com/publication /the-millennials-a-new-generation-of-employees-a-new-set-of -engagement-policies/.
5. Year Up. "Partners." https://www.yearup.org/partners.
6. Year Up. "Research." https://www.yearup.org/about/research.

CHAPTER 1

1. Onibada, Ade. "Brands Have Been Speaking Out About Racism And This One Meme Captures Just How Hollow Some Of Them Are." *Buzzfeed,* June 1, 2020. https://www.buzzfeednews.com /article/adeonibada/generic-brands-george-floyd-protest-statement.
2. Spangler, Todd. "Bon Appétit Rebuilds Video Slate With Eight New Chefs Following Wave of Protest Resignations." Variety, October 13, 2020. https://variety.com/2020/digital/news/bon-appetit-conde -nast-video-hosts-diversity-protest-resignations-1234802407/.
3. Breuninger, Kevin. "NFL bans on-field kneeling during the national anthem." CNBC.com, May 23, 2018. https://www.cnbc.com/2018 /05/23/nfl-bans-on-field-kneeling-during-the-national-anthem.html.

4. McIntosh, Kriston, Emily Moss, Ryan Nunn, and Jay Shambaugh. "Examining the Black-white wealth gap." Brookings, February 27, 2020. https://www.brookings.edu/blog/up-front/2020/02/27/examining-the-black-white-wealth-gap/.

5. Citi. "Citi's *Action for Racial Equity* Initiative Invests $1 Billion to Address the Racial Wealth Gap in the U.S." BusinessWire, November 9, 2021. https://www.businesswire.com/news/home/20211109006099/en/Citi%E2%80%99s-Action-for-Racial-Equity-Initiative-Invests-1-Billion-to-Address-the-Racial-Wealth-Gap-in-the-U.S.

6. Pisani, Bob. "Powerful corporate profits and forecasts of more to come have investors cheering." CNBC, February 5, 2021. https://www.cnbc.com/2021/02/05/powerful-corporate-profits-and-promises-of-more-to-come-have-investors-cheering.html.

7. Edelman. "20 Years of Trust." https://www.edelman.com/20yearsoftrust/04-chapter-2.html.

8. Ibid.

9. Morgan Stanley Institute for Sustainable Investing. "Sustainable Signals: Individual Investor Interest Drive by Impact, Conviction and Choice." 2019.

10. Gilbert, Jay. "The Millennials: A new generation of employees, a new set of engagement policies." *Ivery Business Journal.* September/October 2011. https://iveybusinessjournal.com/publication/the-millennials-a-new-generation-of-employees-a-new-set-of-engagement-policies/.

11. Morgan Stanley Institute for Sustainable Investing. "Sustainable Signals: Individual Investor Interest Drive by Impact, Conviction and Choice." 2019.

12. Stackla. "Bridging the Gap: Consumer & Marketing Perspectives on Content in the Digital Age." https://stackla.com/resources/reports/bridging-the-gap-consumer-marketing-perspectives-on-content-in-the-digital-age/.

13. Reputation. "2020 Retail Reputation Report." https://reputation.com/resources/report/retail-reputation-report/.

14. Nielsen. "The Global, Socially-Conscious Consumer." March 2012. https://www.nielsen.com/us/en/insights/report/2012/the-global—socially-conscious-consumer/.

15. Edelman. "Edelman Trust Barometer 2021." https://www.edelman.com/sites/g/files/aatuss191/files/2021-05/2021%20Edelman%20Trust%20Barometer%20Special%20Report_Business%20and%20Racial%20Justice%20in%20America.pdf.

16. Data sources: Edelman and Nielsen

17. Neumann, Jeff, and Tracey Matsue Loeffelholz. "40 Acres and a Mule Would Be at Least $6.4 Trillion Today—What the U.S. Really Owes Black America." *Yes! Magazine*, Summer 2015. https://www.yesmagazine.org/issues/make-it-right/infographic-40-acres-and-a-mule-would-be-at-least-64-trillion-today/GR201574JTF.jpg.

18. Opportunity Insights. "Neighborhoods." https://opportunityinsights.org/neighborhoods/.

19. Reiff, Nathan. "10 Biggest Companies in the World." *Investopedia*, January 18, 2021. https://www.investopedia.com/articles/active-trading/111115/why-all-worlds-top-10-companies-are-american.asp.

20. Fortune Editors. "The 25 Best Global Companies to Work For." *Fortune*, October 26, 2016. http://fortune.com/2016/10/26/best-global-companies/.

21. Porter, Michael E., and Jan W. Rivkin. "The Looming Challenge to U.S. Competitiveness." *Harvard Business Review*, March 2012. https://hbr.org/2012/03/the-looming-challenge-to-us-competitiveness.

22. Fink, Larry. "The Power of Capitalism." *BlackRock*. https://www.blackrock.com/corporate/investor-relations/larry-fink-ceo-letter.

23. Mull, Amanda. "Brands Have Nothing Real to Say About Racism." *The Atlantic*, June 3, 2020.https://www.theatlantic.com/health/archive/2020/06/brands-racism-protests-amazon-nfl-nike/612613/.

24. Mull, Amanda. "Body Positivity is a Scam." *Vox,* June 5, 2020. https://www.vox.com/2018/6/5/17236212/body-positivity-scam-dove-campaign-ads.

25. Business Roundtable. "Business Roundtable Redefines the Purpose of a Corporation to Promote 'An Economy That Serves All Americans'." August 19, 2019. https://www.businessroundtable.org/business-roundtable-redefines-the-purpose-of-a-corporation-to-promote-an-economy-that-serves-all-americans.

26. The Investment Integration Project. "Addressing systemic social risk: A roadmap for financial system action." December, 2020. https://www.tiiproject.com/wp-content/uploads/2020/12/AddressingSystemicSocialRisk-ARoadmap-12-7-2020_FINAL.pdf.

27. Useem, Jerry. "Beware of Corporate Promises." *The Atlantic*, August 2020. https://www.theatlantic.com/ideas/archive/2020/08/companies-stand-solidarity-are-licensing-themselves-discriminate/614947/.

28. Ibid.

CHAPTER 2

1. Nielsen. "The Global, Socially-Conscious Consumer." March 2012. https://www.nielsen.com/us/en/insights/report/2012/the-global--socially-conscious-consumer/.

2. Stackla. "Bridging the Gap: Consumer & Marketing Perspectives on Content in the Digital Age." https://stackla.com/resources/reports/bridging-the-gap-consumer-marketing-perspectives-on-content-in-the-digital-age/.

3. Fry, Richard. "Millennials overtake Baby Boomers as America's largest generation." Pew Research Center, April 28, 2020. https://www.pewresearch.org/fact-tank/2020/04/28/millennials-overtake-baby-boomers-as-americas-largest-generation/.

4. Merkle. "Millennial Women Are Here to Slay: *Merkle and Levo Release Report Uncovering Buying Behaviors and Purchasing Power of Millennial Women.*" *BusinessWire*, March 8, 2018. https://www.businesswire.com/news/home/20180308005602/en.

5. Coldwell Banker. "A Look at Wealth 2019: Millennial Millionaires." October 16, 2019. https://blog.coldwellbankerluxury.com/a-look-at-wealth-millennial-millionaires/.

6. Morgan Stanley Institute for Sustainable Investing, "Sustainable Signals: Individual Investor Interest Driven by Impact, Conviction and Choice," 2019.

7. Cone. "2015 Cone Communications Millennial CSR Study." https://www.conecomm.com/research-blog/2015-cone-communications-millennial-csr-study.

8. Nielsen. "Millennials on Millennials: US Shopping Insights in a New Era." Fall 2018. https://www.nielsen.com/wp-content/uploads/sites/3/2019/04/millennials-on-millennials-shopping-insights-report.pdf.

9. Merkle. "Millennial Women Are Here to Slay: *Merkle and Levo Release Report Uncovering Buying Behaviors and Purchasing Power of Millennial Women.*" *BusinessWire*, March 8, 2018. https://www.businesswire.com/news/home/20180308005602/en.

10. The Nielsen Company. "Millennials on Millennials: U.S. Shopping Insights in a New Era." Fall 2018, p. 13. https://www.nielsen.com/wp-content/uploads/sites/3/2019/04/millennials-on-millennials-shopping-insights-report.pdf.

11. The Nielsen Company. "Millennials on Millennials.

12. The Nielsen Company. "Millennials on Millennials, p. 13.

13. Frey, William H. "The millennial generation: A demographic bridge to America's diverse future." *Brookings,* January 2018. https://www.brookings.edu/research/millennials/.

14. Nielsen. "Black Impact: Consumer Categories Where African Americans Move Markets." February 15, 2018. https://www.nielsen .com/us/en/insights/article/2018/black-impact-consumer-categories -where-african-americans-move-markets/.

15. Danziger, Pamela N. "Retailers Need To Go Beyond Demographics To Go Big With Their Latino Customers." *Forbes*, October 9, 2019. https://www.forbes.com/sites/pamdanziger/2019/10/09 /why-retailers-need-to-think-big-about-their-latino-customers/?sh= 1ba38efa2b1b.

16. Ibid.

17. Nielsen. "Black Impact: Consumer Categories Where African Americans Move Markets." February 15, 2018. https://www.nielsen .com/us/en/insights/article/2018/black-impact-consumer-categories -where-african-americans-move-markets/.

18. The Urban Institute. "Nine Charts about Wealth Inequality in America." October 5, 2017. https://apps.urban.org/features/wealth -inequality-charts/.

19. Turner, Ani. "Business Case for Racial Equity." W.K. Kellogg Foundation, July 24, 2018. https://www.wkkf.org/resource- directory/resources/2018/07/business-case-for-racial-equity.

20. "Path to 15|55." http://www.pathto1555.org.

21. Athleta. "Our Mission." https://athleta.gap.com/browse/info.do?cid =1074427&mlink=55287,15864962,Footer_Sustainability&clink= 15864962#BCorp.

22. Gap Inc. "Gap Inc. Announces 100 percent Sustainable Cotton Goal." *Businesswire*, June 6, 2019. https://www.businesswire .com/news/home/20190606005196/en/Gap-Inc.-Announces-100 -Sustainable-Cotton-Goal.

23. Ibid.

24. Ibid.

25. SGB Media. "Gap Inc. Snaps Up Athleta for $150 Million." September 29, 2008. https://sgbonline.com/gap-inc-snaps-up -athleta-for-150-million/.

26. Cotopaxi. "About Us." https://www.cotopaxi.com/pages/gear-for -good.

27. The Coca-Cola Company. "Water Conservation." https://www .coca-colacompany.com/sustainable-business/water-stewardship.

28. PepsiCo. "Water." https://www.pepsico.com/sustainability-report /water.

29. In the "Spotlight On" sections in each of the next two chapters, I want to go deeper into things related to specific types of companies or individuals. They may not be relevant to all readers; however, they are important things to consider as you or your company

goes about changing how you make your money in order to create equitable impact.

30. Path to 15|55. "How Usable Capital Will Unleash Black Business Growth." https://www.pathto1555.org/usablecapital.

31. Mizell, Jill. "The American Public Wants Companies to Take Action on Advancing Racial Equity – Especially Black Americans." JustCapital, July 9, 2020. https://justcapital.com/news/the-american -public-wants-companies-to-take-action-on-advancing-racial -equity-especially-black-americans/.

32. Hills, Greg, Lakshmi Iyer, Michael McAfee, Josh Kirschenbaum, and Martin Whittaker. "A CEO Blueprint for Racial Equity." *PolicyLink*. https://www.policylink.org/resources-tools/ceo-blueprint -for-racial-equity.

33. PolicyLink, FSG, and JUST Capital. Corporate Insights into the CEO Blueprint for Racial Equity." https://www.policylink.org/resources -tools/ceo-blueprint-for-racial-equity-2021.

34. Living Cities. "Living Cities Announces Capital Investment in Jacmel Growth Partners to Help Scale Lower Middle Market Businesses While Benefiting Employees and Communities." *PRNewswire*, December 17, 2020. https://www.prnewswire.com /news-releases/living-cities-announces-capital-investment-in-jacmel -growth-partners-to-help-scale-lower-middle-market-businesses -while-benefiting-employees-and-communities-301194639.html.

35. Jacmel Growth Partners. "My Story." https://www.jacmelgp.com /my-story.

36. Jacmel Growth Partners. "Home page." https://www.jacmelgp .com/.

37. Ibid.

CHAPTER 3

1. Nielsen. "The Global, Socially-Conscious Consumer." March 2012. https://www.nielsen.com/us/en/insights/report/2012/the-global --socially-conscious-consumer/.

2. Stackla. "Bridging the Gap: Consumer & Marketing Perspectives on Content in the Digital Age." https://stackla.com/resources/reports /bridging-the-gap-consumer-marketing-perspectives-on-content-in -the-digital-age/.

3. The Urban Institute. "Nine Charts about Wealth Inequality in America." October 5, 2017. https://apps.urban.org/features/wealth -inequality-charts/.

4. The Investment Integration Project. "Confronting Income Inequality." June 2021. https://www.tiiproject.com/wp-content /uploads/2021/06/Confronting-Income-Inequality-Toolkit-TIIP -Updated-6-8-218575.pdf.

5. AEO. "The Tapestry of Black Business Ownership in America." https://aeoworks.org/our-work/cohorts/tapestry-project/.

6. Ibid.

7. National CAPACD. "Small Business, Big Dreams." 2019. https://www.nationalcapacd.org/data-research/small-business-big-dreams/.

8. Black Enterprise Editors. "50 of the nation's top black women business owners join forces." *Black Enterprise,* January 25, 2022. https://www.blackenterprise.com/50-of-the-nations-top-black-women-business-owners-join-forces/.

9. Ibid.

10. Ibid.

11. The Hackett Group. "2021 Supplier Diversity Study." May 2021. https://www.thehackettgroup.com/supplier-diversity-infographic-2105/.

12. Lutz, Ashley. "How McDonald's Inadvertently Created a Huge Competitor in Chipotle." *Insider,* September 18, 2014. https://www.businessinsider.com/mcdonalds-investing-in-chipotle-2014-9.

13. Morgan Stanley Institute for Sustainable Investing. "Sustainable Signals: Individual Investor Interest Driven by Impact, Conviction and Choice." 2019.

14. Doron, Karen. "CalSTRS Board commits to net zero investment portfolio." *CalSTRS,* September 1, 2021. https://www.calstrs.com/news-release/calstrs-board-commits-net-zero-investment-portfolio.

15. Mudaliar, Abhilash, and Rachel Bass. "Evidence on the Financial Performance of Impact Investments." The Global Impact Investing Network, 2017. https://thegiin.org/assets/2017_GIIN_FinancialPerformanceImpactInvestments_Web.pdf.

16. AEO. "The Tapestry of Black Business Ownership in America." https://aeoworks.org/our-work/cohorts/tapestry-project/.

17. Omar, Hafizah. "Decolonizing Lunch Part I: Interrogating our Org Culture Around Food." Living Cities, September 5, 2019. https://livingcities.org/blog/1380-decolonizing-lunch-part-i-interrogating-our-org-culture-around-food.

18. Walmart. "Product Supply Chains: Sustainability Overview." https://corporate.walmart.com/esgreport/esg-issues/product-supply-chain-sustainability.

19. CEO Action for Diversity and Inclusion. "Actions." https://www.ceoaction.com/actions/?Sort=Alphabet&categories=1552#js-filters-container.

20. Path to 15|55. "How Usable Capital Will Unleash Black Business Growth." https://www.pathto1555.org/usablecapital.

21. Parilla, Joseph, and Darrin Redus. "How a new Minority Business Accelerator grant program can close the racial entrepreneurship

gap." *Brookings*, December 9, 2020. https://www.brookings.edu /research/how-a-new-minority-business-accelerator-grant-program -can-close-the-racial-entrepreneurship-gap/?amp.

22. Ibid.

23. Ibid.

24. CincinnatiUSA Regional Chamber. "2017-2018 Annual Review and Strategic Outlook: Minority Business Accelerator." https://www .cincinnatichamber.com/docs/default-source/default-document -library/minority-business-accelerator-files/minority-business -accelerator-annual-report-1718.pd.

25. New Orleans Business Alliance. "2018-2019 Annual Impact Report." https://www.nolaba.org/wp-content/uploads/NOLABA _AnnualReport_2018-2019.pdf.

26. The Data Center. "Who Lives in New Orleans and Metro Parishes Now?" July 28, 2021. https://www.datacenterresearch.org/data -resources/who-lives-in-new-orleans-now/.

27. Hamel, Liz, Jamie Firth, and Mollyann Brodie. "New Orleans Ten Years After the Storm: The Kaiser Family Foundation Katrina Survey Project." Kaiser Family Foundation, August 10, 2015. https://www.kff.org/report-section/new-orleans-ten-years-after-the -storm-section-2/.

28. New Orleans Business Alliance. "2018-2019 Annual Impact Report." https://www.nolaba.org/wp-content/uploads/NOLABA _AnnualReport_2018-2019.pdf.

29. Myers, Ben. "The New Orleans City Council ratifies $15 hourly minimum wage for city workers." *NOLA.com*, October 7, 2021. https://www.nola.com/news/politics/article_d5d8683a-2799-11ec -ad7b-9f8f99f34cce.html.

30. New Orleans Business Alliance. "Impact." https://www.nolaba.org /impact/.

CHAPTER 4

1. Heinz, Kate. "The True Costs of Employee Turnover." *Bullitin*, January 11, 2022. https://builtin.com/recruiting/cost-of-turnover.

2. King, Stephen. "More Than You Think: The Cost of Employee Turnover." GrowthForce. https://www.growthforce.com/blog/the -real-cost-of-employee-turnover-its-more-than-you-think.

3. Work Institute. "2017 Retention Report." http://info.workinstitute .com/retentionreport2017.

4. McFeely, Shane, and Ben Wiger. "This Fixable Problem Costs U.S. Businesses $1 Trillion," Gallup, March 13, 2019. https://www .gallup.com/workplace/247391/fixable-problem-costs-businesses -trillion.aspx.

5. Gallup. "Employee Engagement." https://www.gallup.com/workplace/229424/employee-engagement.aspx.

6. Adkins, Amy. "Millennials: The Job-Hopping Generation." *Gallup.* https://www.gallup.com/workplace/231587/millennials-job-hopping-generation.aspx.

7. TERRA Staffing Group. "The Real Cost of Employee Turnover in 2021." https://www.terrastaffinggroup.com/resources/blog/cost-of-employee-turnover/.

8. McQueen, Nina. "Workplace Culture Trends: The Key to Hiring (and Keeping) Top Talent in 2018." LinkedIn, June 26, 2018. https://blog.linkedin.com/2018/june/26/workplace-culture-trends-the-key-to-hiring-and-keeping-top-talent.

9. Korolevich, Sara. "The State of Remote Work In 2021: A Survey of the American Workforce." *GoodHire*, October 27, 2021. https://www.goodhire.com/resources/articles/state-of-remote-work-survey/.

10. Cavalluzzi, Alessandra. "How Community Involvement Can Boost Employee Engagement." *SHRM,* July 18, 2018. https://www.shrm.org/hr-today/news/hr-magazine/book-blog/pages/how-community-involvement-can-boost-employee-engagement.aspx.

11. McQueen, Nina. "Workplace Culture Trends: The Key to Hiring (and Keeping) Top Talent in 2018." LinkedIn, June 26, 2018. https://blog.linkedin.com/2018/june/26/workplace-culture-trends-the-key-to-hiring-and-keeping-top-talent.

12. Net Impact. "Talent Report: What Workers Want in 2012." https://www.netimpact.org/sites/default/files/documents/what-workers-want-2012-summary.pdf.

13. Ibid.

14. Deloitte. "Deloitte Volunteer IMPACT Survey." 2011. https://www2.deloitte.com/content/dam/Deloitte/us/Documents/us-citizenship-2011-impact-survey-employee-engagement.pdf.

15. Net Impact. "Talent Report: What Workers Want in 2012." https://www.netimpact.org/sites/default/files/documents/what-workers-want-2012-summary.pdf.

16. DKB Foundation. "Home page." https://dkbfoundation.org/.

17. The State of Illinois. "Illinois Results First: The High Cost of Incarceration." Summer 2018. https://spac.icjia-api.cloud/uploads/Illinois_Result_First-The_High_Cost_of_Recidivism_2018-20191106T18123262.pdf.

18. Greyston Bakery. "The Case for Open Hiring." https://www.greyston.org/the-case-for-open-hiring.

19. DKB Foundation. "Home page." https://dkbfoundation.org/.

20. Rivera, Lauren A. "Hiring as Cultural Matching: The Case of Elite Professional Service Firms." *American Sociological Review* 77, no. 6 (December 2012): 999–1022. https://doi.org/10.1177/0003122412463213.

21. Lorenzo, Rocío, Nicole Voigt, Miki Tsusaka, Matt Krentz, and Katie Abouzahr. "How Diverse Leadership Teams Boost Innovation." *BCG*, January 23, 2018. https://www.bcg.com/en-gb/publications/2018/how-diverse-leadership-teams-boost-innovation.

22. Edelman. "Edelman Trust Barometer 2021." https://www.edelman.com/sites/g/files/aatuss191/files/2021-05/2021%20Edelman%20Trust%20Barometer%20Special%20Report_Business%20and%20Racial%20Justice%20in%20America.pdf.

23. Korn Ferry. "The Future of Work Trends in 2022." https://www.kornferry.com/insights/featured-topics/future-of-work/2022-future-of-work-trends.

24. Xido, Amanda. "Hybrid work can hurt or help DEI efforts. Here's how to get it right." *FastCompany*, January 27, 2022. https://www.fastcompany.com/90716439/hybrid-work-can-hurt-or-help-dei-efforts-heres-how-to-get-it-right.

25. Korolevich, Sara. "The State of Remote Work in 2021: A Survey of the American Workforce." GoodHire, October 27, 2021. https://www.goodhire.com/resources/articles/state-of-remote-work-survey/.

26. Income Advance Guide, https://www.incomeadvance.org/.

27. National Conference of State Legislatures. "Breastfeeding State Laws." August 26, 2021. https://www.ncsl.org/research/health/breastfeeding-state-laws.aspx.

28. Gilsdorf, Kimberly, and Fay Hanleybrown. "Investing in Entry-Level Talent." FSG. https://www.fsg.org/publications/investing-entry-level-talent.

29. Ibid.

30. Ibid.

31. i4cp. "Developing America's Frontline Workers." https://www.shcoe.org/wp-content/uploads/2016/02/Developing-Americas-Frontline-Workers-i4cp-UpSkill-America-2016.pdf.

32. Hanleybrown, Fay, Lakshmi Iyer, Josh Kirschenbaum, Sandra Medrano, and Aaron Mihaly. "Advancing Frontline Employees of Color." FSG. https://www.fsg.org/publications/advancing-frontline-employees-color.

33. Ibid.

34. Talent Rewire. "Caterpillar, Inc." https://www.talentrewire.org/innovation-story/caterpillar-inc/.

35. i4cp. "Developing America's Frontline Workers." https://www
    .shcoe.org/wp-content/uploads/2016/02/Developing-Americas
    -Frontline-Workers-i4cp-UpSkill-America-2016.pdf.
36. National Low Income Housing Coalition. "Out of Reach 2021."
    https://reports.nlihc.org/oor.
37. Paycor. "Minimum Wage by State and 2022 Increases." November
    29, 2021. https://www.paycor.com/resource-center/articles/minimum
    -wage-by-state/.
38. Ramsey Solutions. "The Cost of Living in California." December 3,
    2021. https://www.ramseysolutions.com/real-estate/cost-of-living
    -in-california.
39. Center for American Progress. "Quick Facts About the Gender
    Wage Gap." March 24, 2020. https://www.americanprogress.org
    /issues/women/reports/2020/03/24/482141/quick-facts-gender-wage
    -gap/.
40. Patten, Eileen. "Racial, gender wage gaps persist in U.S. despite
    some progress." Pew Research Center, July 1, 2016. https://www
    .pewresearch.org/fact-tank/2016/07/01/racial-gender-wage-gaps
    -persist-in-u-s-despite-some-progress/.
41. Irwin, Neil. "To Understand Rising Inequality, Consider the
    Janitors at Two Top Companies, Then and Now." *New York Times*,
    September 3, 2017. https://www.nytimes.com/2017/09/03/upshot
    /to-understand-rising-inequality-consider-the-janitors-at-two-top
    -companies-then-and-now.html.
42. Davis, Alyssa, and Lawrence Mishel. "Runaway CEO pay in
    30 seconds." Economic Policy Institute. https://www.epi.org
    /multimedia/runaway-ceo-pay-30-seconds/.
43. Lean In. "What Companies Can Do About Equal Pay." https://
    leanin.org/what-companies-can-do-about-equal-pay#!
44. Money Management Institute. "MMI/FundFire Survey Highlights
    Racial Diversity Gaps Across Asset Management Industry."
    November 8, 2017. https://www.mminst.org/press-releases
    /mmifundfire-survey-highlights-racial-diversity-gaps-across-asset
    -management-industry.
45. Knight Foundation. "Diversifying Investments: A Study of
    Ownership Diversity and Performance in the Asset Management
    Industry." January 28, 2019. https://knightfoundation.org/reports
    /diversifying-investments-a-study-of-ownership-diversity-and
    -performance-in-the-asset-management-industry/.
46. Lyons-Padilla, Sarah, et al. 2019. "Race influences professional
    investors' financial judgments." *Proceedings of the National
    Academy of Sciences of the United States of America*, vol. 116, 35
    (2019): 17225-17230. doi:10.1073/pnas.1822052116.

47. Austermuhle, Martin. "First Walmart Stores In D.C. To Open Dec. 4, Will Employ 600 People." WAMU, November 19, 2013. https://wamu.org/story/13/11/19/first_walmart_stores_in_dc_to_open_dec_4/.

48. Freed, Benjamin. "Days After Beating 'Living Wage' Bill, Walmart Will Start Hiring for DC Stores." Washingtonian, September 19, 2013. https://www.washingtonian.com/2013/09/19/days-after-beating-living-wage-bill-walmart-will-start-hiring-for-dc-stores/#.

49. HR&A. "Economic and Fiscal Impacts of Walmart on Washington, DC." January 2015. https://www.scribd.com/document/259171038/Walmart-Economic-Impact-Study.

50. Ibid.

51. Neibauer, Michael. "Wal-Mart's first year in D.C., by the numbers." *Washington Business Journal*, March 18, 2015. https://www.bizjournals.com/washington/breaking_ground/2015/03/wal-marts-first-year-in-d-c-by-the-numbers.html.

52. Walmart. "Center for Racial Equity." https://walmart.org/diversity-equity-and-inclusion/center-for-racial-equity.

53. Walmart. "Human capital: Good jobs and advancement for associates." https://corporate.walmart.com/esgreport/esg-issues/human-capital.

54. Walmart. "2019 Environmental, Social and Governance Report." https://corporate.walmart.com/media-library/document/2019-environmental-social-governance-report/_proxyDocument?id=0000016c-20b5-d46a-afff-f5bdafd30000.

55. Corkery, Michael. "Walmart will raise hourly pay for 565,000 workers." *New York Times*, September 2, 2021. https://www.nytimes.com/2021/09/02/business/walmart-hourly-pay-raise.html.

CHAPTER 5

1. Of course, there is so much more to learn than I can fit into one book. There are a plethora of books, conferences, classes, and other resources that can help you and your staff bone up on what it takes to create financial and social returns at the same time.

2. Hartel, Heather. "This New York bakery wants to teach its 'open hiring' practices to other companies." *New York Business Journal*, July 6, 2018. https://www.bizjournals.com/newyork/news/2018/07/06/this-new-york-bakery-wants-to-teach-itsopen-hiring.html.

3. Connley, Courtney. "Why the CEO of Basecamp only allows employees to work 32 hours a week." *CNBC*, August 4, 2017. https://www.cnbc.com/2017/08/03/the-ceo-of-basecamp-only-allows-employees-to-put-in-a-32-hour-workweek.html.

4. Basecamp. "About." https://basecamp.com/about.

5. Athleta. "About Us." https://athleta.gap.com/browse/info.do?cid=1
   074427&mlink=1074427,15886559,Footer_BrandAmbassadors&c
   link=15886559#Ambassadors.
6. Gliffy. "How Tribal Leadership Evolves in the Real World."
   October 9, 2017. https://www.gliffy.com/blog/how-tribal
   -leadership-evolves-in-the-real-world.
7. Meadows, Donella. *Thinking In Systems: A Primer*. Chelsea Green
   Publishing, 2008.
8. Kania, John, Mark Kramer, and Peter Senge. "The Water
   of Systems Change." FSG, May 2018. https://www.fsg.org
   /publications/water_of_systems_change.
9. Ibid.
10. Ibid.

INDEX

ABOUT THE AUTHOR

As an entrepreneur, Six Sigma Black Belt, and technologist, Tynesia is uniquely positioned to catalyze a results-driven era of social change. She has been religiously leading and writing about enterprises that "do well and do good" for over a decade.

As president and CEO of CapEQ™, which she founded in 2011, she demonstrated how business and community goals can align toward mutual outcomes, helping Fortune 500 clients like the Carlyle Group, Marriott, and others change the way the world does business. In her previous role as chief impact officer of Living Cities, Tynesia was responsible for ensuring that $100 million of investment produced outcomes that improved the lives of people across the country. In her first book, *Just Change: How to Collaborate for Lasting Impact*, Tynesia shares her experience investing in cities and leaders across the country.

Tynesia leveraged effective cross-sector partnerships to help establish the Social Innovation Fund and the Workforce Investment and Opportunity Act. As founding executive director of Year Up National Capital Region (NCR) she raised $20 million, was recognized by President Obama, and supported the organization to ensure that thousands of low-income young adults are hired in careers with family-sustaining wages.

Tynesia has been a featured speaker at events ranging from South by Southwest to the White House Council for

Community Solutions. She has published articles featured in the *Washington Post, Forbes*, and more, and her work was highlighted in the *New York Times* bestseller *A Year Up.*

Tynesia received her MBA from Harvard Business School and has a dual degree in Electrical Engineering and Computer Science from Duke University. She and her college sweetheart, Keith, are committed to indoctrinating their children, Dylan and Sydney, with a love of Duke basketball and all things geeky and sci-fi.